William N. Sheats

Digest and Compilation of the School Laws of the State of Florida

With the Forms, Regulations and Instructions of the Department of Education

William N. Sheats

Digest and Compilation of the School Laws of the State of Florida
With the Forms, Regulations and Instructions of the Department of Education

ISBN/EAN: 9783337187699

Printed in Europe, USA, Canada, Australia, Japan

Cover: Foto ©ninafisch / pixelio.de

More available books at **www.hansebooks.com**

DIGEST AND COMPILATION

OF THE

SCHOOL LAWS

OF THE

STATE OF FLORIDA,

WITH THE

FORMS, REGULATIONS AND INSTRUCTIONS OF THE DEPARTMENT OF EDUCATION.

COMPILED BY

WILLIAM N. SHEATS,

SUPERINTENDENT OF PUBLIC INSTRUCTION.

TALLAHASSEE, FLA.:
PRINTED AT THE TALLAHASSEEAN BOOK AND JOB OFFICE.
1893.

STATE BOARD OF EDUCATION.

(EX-OFFICIO.)

Hon. H. L. MITCHELL, Governor, President.

Hon. JOHN L. CRAWFORD, Secretary of State.

Hon. WILLIAM B. LAMAR, Attorney-General.

Hon. C. B. COLLINS, State Treasurer.

Hon. WILLIAM N. SHEATS, Superintendent of Public Instruction, Secretary.

CONSTITUTION OF FLORIDA.

ARTICLE XII.

EDUCATION.

SECTION 1. The Legislature shall provide for a uniform system of public free schools, and shall provide for the liberal maintenance of the same. Duty of Legislature.

SEC. 2. There shall be a Superintendent of Public Instruction, whose duties shall be prescribed by law, and whose term of office shall be four years and until the election and qualification of his successor. Term of office of Supt. Pub. Inst.

SEC. 3. The Governor, Secretary of State, Attorney-General, State Treasurer and State Superintendent of Public Instruction shall constitute a body corporate, to be known as the State Board of Education of Florida, of which the Governor shall be President, and the Superintendent of Public Instruction Secretary. This Board shall have power to remove any subordinate school officer for cause, upon notice to the incumbent; and shall have the management and investment of all State School Funds under such regulations as may be prescribed by law, and such supervision of schools of higher grades as the law shall provide. Personnel and powers of State Board of Education.

SEC. 4. The State School Fund, the interest of which shall be exclusively applied to the support and maintenance of public free schools, shall be derived from the following sources: Interest only to be applied.

The proceeds of all lands that have been or may hereafter be granted to the State by the United States for public school purposes. Sources of State School Fund.

Donations to the State when the purpose is not specified.

Appropriations by the State.

The proceeds of escheated property or forfeitures.

Twenty-five per cent. of the sales of public lands which are now or may hereafter be owned by the State.

SCHOOL LAWS.

1893.

Principal inviolate.

SEC. 5. The principal of the State School Fund shall remain sacred and inviolate.

One Mill Tax

SEC. 6. A special tax of one mill on the dollar of all taxable property in the State, in addition to the other means provided, shall be levied and apportioned annually for the support and maintenance of public free schools.

Basis of apportionment of One Mill Tax and interest on State School Fund.

SEC. 7. Provision shall be made by law for the distribution of the interest on the State School Fund and the special tax among the several counties of the State in proportion to the number of children residing therein between the ages of six and twenty-one years.*

County School Tax.

SEC. 8. Each county shall be required to assess and collect annually for the support of public free schools therein, a tax of not less than three mills nor more than five mills on the dollar on all taxable property in the same.

County School Fund; whence derived and how disbursed.

SEC. 9. The County School Fund shall consist, in addition to the tax provided for in Section Eight of this Article, of the proportion of the interest of the State School Fund and of the one mill State tax apportioned to the county; the net proceeds of all fines collected under the penal laws of the State within the county; all capitation taxes collected within the county; and shall be disbursed by the County Board of Public Instruction solely for the maintenance and support of public free schools.

Provisions for School District.

School Trustees.

District Tax.

SEC. 10. The Legislature may provide for the division of any county or counties into convenient school districts; and for the election biennially of three school trustees, who shall hold their office for two years, and who shall have the supervision of all the schools within the district; and for the levying and collection of a district school tax, for the exclusive use of public free schools within the district, whenever a majority of the qualified electors thereof that pay a tax on real or personal property shall vote in favor of such levy; *Provided*, That any tax authorized by this section shall not exceed three mills on the dollar in any one year on the taxable property of the district.

Town or city may be a School District.

Disbursement of District Fund.

SEC. 11. Any incorporated town or city may constitute a School District. The fund raised by Section Ten may be expended in the district where levied for building or repairing school houses, for the purchase of school libraries and text-books, for salaries of teachers, or for other educational purposes, so that the distribution among all the schools of the district be equitable.

*See proposed Amendment to this Section.

SCHOOL LAWS.

SEC. 12. White and colored children shall not be taught in the same school, but impartial provision shall be made for both.

1893. Separate schools for negroes.

SEC. 13. No law shall be enacted authorizing the diversion or the lending of any county or district school funds, or the appropriation of any part of the permanent or available school fund to any other than school purposes; nor shall the same, or any part thereof, be appropriated to or used for the support of any sectarian school.

Prohibitions concerning School Fund.

SEC. 14. The Legislature at its first session shall provide for the establishment, maintenance and management of such Normal Schools, not to exceed two, as the interests of public education may demand.

Normal Schools.

SEC. 15. The compensation of all county school officers shall be paid from the school fund of their respective counties, and all other county officers receiving stated salaries shall be paid from the general funds of their respectives counties.

Compensation of school officers.

ARTICLE IV.

SEC. 25. The Superintendent of Public Instruction shall have supervision of all matters pertaining to public instruction; the supervision of State buildings devoted to educational purposes, and perform such other duties as the Legislature may provide by law.

Powers and duties of State Superintendent. Sec. 25, Art. IV, Const.

SEC. 27. * * * * * * * [He] shall make a full report of his official acts, of the receipts and expenditures of his office, and of the requirements of the same, to the Governor at the beginning of each regular session of the Legislature, or whenever the Governor shall require it. Such * * * [report] shall be laid before the Legislature by the Governor at the beginning of each regular session thereof. Either house of the Legislature may at any time call upon * * * * * * * * [him] for information required by it.

Shall make report.

Abbr. Sec. 27, Art. IV, Const.

HOUSE JOINT RESOLUTION Proposing an Amendment to the Constitution of the State of Florida.

Be it resolved by the Legislature of the State of Florida:

That the following amendment to the Constitution of the State of Florida be, and the same is hereby agreed to, and shall be submitted to the electors of the State at the general election in October, A. D. 1894, for ratification or rejection:

Amendment to Sec. 7, Art. XII of the Constitution.

1893.

Aprotionmento: School Fund.

Section 7, of Article XII, of the Constitution, is hereby amended so as to read as follows:

SECTION 7. Provision shall be made by law for the apportionment and distribution of the interest on the State School Fund and all other means provided, including the special tax for the support and maintenance of public free schools, among the several counties of the State in proportion to the average attendance upon schools in the said counties respectively.

Approved June 2, 1893.

SCHOOL LAWS

OF THE

STATE OF FLORIDA,

AS COMPILED

From the Revised Statutes, and the Acts of the Legislature of 1893.

GENERAL PROVISIONS.

1. There shall be established and maintained a uniform system of public instruction free to all the youth residing in the State between the ages of six (6) and twenty-one (21) years, as far as the funds will admit, as hereinafter provided. *Uniform System of Public Instruction. School age. Rev. Stat. Sec. 225.*

2. The officers of the Department of Public Instruction shall be a State Superintendent of Public Instruction, a State Board of Education, a Board of Public Instruction for each county, a Superintendent of Public Instruction for each county, local School Supervisors and Treasurers. *Officers. Ibid Sec. 226.*

3. I. All such officers who shall hold their offices by statute shall conform to the regulations of the Department of Public Instruction. *Subject to regulations.*

II. They shall retain their offices during the faithful performance of their duties, but not to exceed four years at any time. *Tenure of office. Ibid, Sec. 229.*

III. They shall be subject to removal for incompetency, neglect of duty, or any cause which would disqualify them for the positions if not incumbents. *Subject to removal.*

4. No officer shall vote on a question fixing his own compensation. *When not to vote. Ibid, Sec. 230.*

5. A majority of any educational board shall constitute a quorum for the transaction of business. *A quorum. Ibid, Sec. 231.*

GENERAL DUTIES OF OFFICERS.

6. Every school officer who shall be appointed under statutory provision, is required:

School officers to qualify.
Ibid, Sec. 232.

I. Before entering upon the duties of his office, and within ten days after receiving notice of his appointment, to subscribe to an acceptance of the appointment and to pledge that he will faithfully perform the duties of the position, and to forward the same with his postoffice address to the State Superintendent of Public Instruction.

To give bond with sureties.

II. Before receiving any school moneys or property of any kind, for safe keeping or disbursement, to give bond, with two good sureties, the bonds to be fixed and approved by the Board of Public Instruction for the county, the original to be filed in the office of the Clerk of the Circuit Court, and a certified copy to be held by the officer giving the security, to be produced when required.

Liability for loss.

III. Any officer in charge of school moneys or property to be so disbursed, shall satisfy himself that the officer to whom he issues it has given bond as aforesaid, or be personally liable for any loss in consequence of such neglect.

To turn over effects to successor.
Ibid, Sec 233.

IV. Every officer shall turn over to his successor in office, on retiring, all books, papers, documents, funds, moneys and property of whatever kind, which he may have acquired, received and held by virtue of his office, and take full receipts for them of his successor.

STATE BOARD OF EDUCATION.

Constitution of. Ib., 234.

7. The State Board of Education shall consist of the Governor, the Secretary of State, the Attorney-General, the State Treasurer and the State Superintendent of Public Instruction. The Governor shall be the President, the State Treasurer shall be the Treasurer, and the State Superintendent of Public Instruction the Secretary of said Board. Said Board is a body corporate, with full power to perform all corporate acts for educational purposes.

A body corporate.

Powers and duties. Ib. 235.

8. The State Board of Education are directed and empowered:

With regard to school lands.

I. To obtain possession of and take the charge, oversight and management of all lands granted to or held by the State for educational purposes, and to fix the terms of sale, rental or use of such lands, and to do whatever may be necessary to preserve them from trespass or injury, and for their improvement.

SCHOOL LAWS.

II. To have the direction and management, and provide for the safe keeping and expenditure of all the educational funds of the State, with due regard to the highest interests of education. *1893. With regard to School Fund.*

III. To entertain and decide upon questions and appeals referred to them by the State Superintendent of Public Instruction on any matter of difference or dispute arising under the operations of this act, and to prescribe the manner of making appeals and conducting arbitrations. *With regard to appeals.*

IV. To remove any subordinate officer in the department for incompetency, neglect of duty or other cause which would disqualify a person for the appointment. *Removal of subordinate officers.*

V. To keep in view the establishment of schools on a broad and liberal basis, the object of which shall be to impart instruction to youth in the profession of teaching, in the knowledge of the natural sciences, the theory and practice of agriculture, horticulture, mining, engineering and the mechanic arts, in the ancient and modern languages, in the higher range of mathematics, literature, and in useful and ornamental branches not taught in common schools. *Higher Education.*

VI. To co-operate with the State Superintendent of Public Instruction in the management of the department, and in the general diffusion of knowledge in the State. *To co-operate with State Superintendent of Public Instruction.*

VII. The Board of Education shall invest moneys of the common school fund which it may now have, and which from time to time may come to its hands, in bonds of the United States and of the several states at the current market values of such bonds at the time of making such investments, and such Board may from time to time change investments held by it, and reinvest the proceeds arising from such change in securities authorized by law: *Provided, however,* That in no case shall any investment be made in any bonds on which the interest is not regularly paid, or as to the validity of which any suit may be pending. *To invest School Fund. Ib., 267. Investment in what.*

VIII. On nomination by the State Superintendent of Public Instruction, the State Board of Education shall appoint members to fill all vacancies for unexpired terms on County School Boards [County Boards of Public Instruction]. *To fill vacancies on County School Boards. Abbreviation of Sec. 4, Chap. 4196, June 2, '93.*

NORMAL SCHOOLS.

9. A Normal School for the training and instruction of white teachers is established at DeFuniak Springs, Walton county, under the direction and control of the State Board of Education. *White Normal established. Ib., Sec. 268.*

SCHOOL LAWS.

1893.

Faculty, how elected.

10. The State Board of Education shall elect a faculty, to consist of a principal and two assistant instructors, who shall have in charge the training and instruction of all students, subject to the approval of the State Board of Education.

Normal School for negroes, established. &c Ib., Sec. 269.

11. A Normal School for colored teachers is established at Tallahassee, Leon county, similar in all respects as prescribed above for the establishment of the normal school for white teachers, and subject to the direction and control of the State Board of Education.

INSTITUTE FOR BLIND, DEAF AND DUMB.

State Board of Education Managers. R. S., Sec. 270.

12. The members of the State Board of Education are the trustees of the institute hereinafter specified, under the name of the Board of Managers of the Florida Institute for the Blind, Deaf and Dumb.

Location. Ib., 271.

13. Said institute shall remain in its present location near St. Augustine, in St. Johns county, and shall be an asylum for the indigent blind and deaf and dumb in this State.

Who are beneficiaries. Ib., 272.

14. Said Board of Managers shall provide for the education, care and maintenance at said asylum of all persons residing in this State between the ages of six and twenty-one years, who may be blind or deaf and dumb, and who are not able to educate and maintain themselves; but any person who may be blind or deaf and dumb, but who may have sufficient means to educate himself, shall be received and cared for in said institution, and enjoy the advantages thereof, by paying such an amount per annum as may be necessary to cover the actual cost of his education and support.

Who shall pay.

Certificate necessary to admit beneficiaries. Ib. 273.

15. Any person entitled to admission into said institute as a non-paying inmate, or the parent, guardian, or next friend of such person, may apply to the Board of County Commissioners of the county of his residence, and the County Commissioners, if satisfied that the person is so entitled to such admission, shall issue a certificate to that effect, upon which the applicant shall be received into the asylum.

Transportation. Ib., 274.

16. Said Board of County Commissioners shall supply means of transportation of such person to said asylum.

Necessary to be provided. Ib., 275.

17. Said Board of Managers shall provide for the inmates of said institute necessary bedding, clothing, food and medical attendance, and such other things as may be proper for the health and comfort of said inmates.

Teachers. Ib., 276.

18. Said Board of Managers shall also provide for the education of the inmates of said institute and shall employ such teachers as may be competent to instruct the blind and deaf

SCHOOL LAWS.

1893.

and dumb, and fit them for aiding in earning a support, and in sharing the enjoyments of life.

19. Said Board of Managers shall report to the Legislature at each session the condition and management of said institute, the work done therein and the expenditures therefor.

Report. Ib., 277

STATE SUPERINTENDENT OF PUBLIC INSTRUCTION.

20. The State Superintendent of Public Instruction shall have the oversight, charge and management of all matters pertaining to public schools, school buildings and grounds.

Jurisdiction of State Supt. Ibid, Sec. 132.

21. It is his duty and he is hereby empowered:

Duties of. Ibid, Sec. 133.

I. To prepare and cause to be printed and distributed gratuitously to Boards of Public Instruction, and other officers and teachers, as many copies of the school laws, and such forms, instruments, instructions, regulations and decisions as he may judge necessary for their use.

Print and distribute laws, forms, etc.

II. To call conventions of County Superintendents of Public Instruction, and other officers, for obtaining and imparting information on the practical workings of the school system, and the means of promoting its efficiency and usefulness.

To call Conventions of County Superintendents.

III. To assemble teachers in institutes and employ competent instructors to impart information on improved methods of teaching and conducting schools, and other relevant matters.

To hold Teachers' Institutes.

IV. To apportion the interest on the common school fund and the fund raised by the one mill State tax authorized by Section 6 of Article XII, of the Constitution, among the several counties of the State in proportion to the number of children residing therein between the ages of six (6) and twenty-one (21) years.

To apportion school moneys.

V. To make such apportionments as may in his judgment be right and just, when the census and returns on which the apportionments should be made are manifestly defective or have not been received by him.

To make discretionary apportionments.

VI. To entertain and decide upon appeals and questions arising under this act, or refer such to the Board of Education for decision.

To decide upon appeals.

VII. To prescribe rules and regulations for the management of the Department of Public Instruction.

To prescribe regulations.

1893.

VIII. He shall have a seal for his office, with which, in connection with his own signature, to authenticate copies of decisions, acts or documents, which copies so authenticated shall be of the same force as the originals.

To have a seal.
Ib., Sec. 134.

IX. He shall reside at the seat of government of this State, and shall keep his office in a room in the capitol.

To reside at Capitol.
Ib., Sec. 135.

X. He shall prepare the questions for county examinations and distribute same to County Superintendents; hold written examinations for and issue State Certificates. He may grant Life Certificates and Special Life Certificates according to law; and may order county examinations on other days than those prescribed by law.

To prepare questions, hold examinations and issue certificates.

Abbr. Secs 8, 9, 10, 20, Chap. 4192, June 8, '93

XI. He shall nominate to the State Board of Education for appointment members to fill all vacancies for unexpired terms on County School Boards [County Boards of Public Instruction].

To nominate for vacancies on County School Board.

Abbr. Sec. 4, Chap. 4193, June 2, 1893.

XII. It shall be the duty of the State Superintendent to visit each seminary at least once in each year, and he shall annually make to the Governor, to be by him laid before the Legislature at each regular session thereof, a full and detailed report of the doings of the respective boards of education, and of all their expenditures, and the moneys received for tuition, and the prospects, progress and usefulness of said seminaries, including so much of the report of the Board of Visitors as he may deem advisable.

Visit Seminaries. Abbr. Sec. 312, 323, Rev. Stat.

Report to the Governor.

COUNTY BOARD OF PUBLIC INSTRUCTION.

22. Each Board of Public Instruction is constituted a body corporate by the name of "The Board of Public Instruction for the County of —————, State of Florida," and in that name may acquire and hold real and personal property, receive bequests and donations, and perform other corporate acts for educational purposes.

A corporate body.
R. S., Sec. 236.

23. Each board shall, before proceeding to any other business, complete its own organization. Then the chairman and secretary shall make and sign two copies of the proceedings of organization, and annex their affidavits to each that the same is a correct and true copy of the original. They shall file one copy in the office of the Clerk of the Circuit Court of the county, to be by him recorded in the record of deeds, and file the other copy in the office of the State Superintendent of Public Instruction.

Organization a primary duty.
Ibid, 241.

SCHOOL LAWS.

24. The title to the school property of the county shall be vested in them and their successors in office, except in such sub-districts as provided for.

1893.
To hold titles Ibid., 237.

25. The members of the Board of Public Instruction shall be paid from the school funds for their services two dollars per diem and ten cents mileage.

Compensation Ibid., 238.

[Mileage from January, 1895, "not exceeding five cents per mile," Sec. 5, Chap. 4193 June 2, 1893].

26. The County Superintendent of Public Instruction shall be secretary of the board.

Secretary of

27. The county treasurers of the several counties shall be and the same are hereby constituted the treasurers of the school funds in their respective counties.

Treasurer of Ib., Sec. 240.

28. Each Board of Public Instruction is directed—

R. S., Sec. 42.

I. To obtain possession of, accept and hold, under proper title, as a corporation, all property possessed, acquired or held by the county for educational purposes, and to manage and dispose of the same for the best interest of education; *Provided*, That nothing in this act shall be so construed as to prevent any sub-district from holding school property that it has, or may hereafter acquire, for school purposes, or prevent such districts from receiving their portion of moneys as set apart for school purposes.

To hold titles and dispose of property.

Sub-district property.

II. To locate and maintain schools in every locality in the county where they may be needed, to accommodate, as far as practicable, all the youth between the ages of six (6) and twenty-one (21) years, during not less than four months in each year.

To locate schools.

School age and minimum term defined.

III. To appoint one supervisor for each school on the recommendation of the patrons, whose duty it shall be to supervise the work of the school and to report to the County Superintendent of Public Instruction monthly the result of his observations.

To appoint Supervisors.

IV. To select and provide a site for each school house of not less than one-half acre of ground in the rural districts, and as nearly that amount as practicable in the villages or cities; the situation to be dry, airy, healthful and pleasant, also reasonably central and convenient of access for all who should attend the school.

Provide school site.

V. To do whatever is necessary with regard to purchasing or renting school sites and premises, constructing, repairing, furnishing, warming, ventilating, keeping in order or improving the school houses, outbuildings, fences, land and movable property, procuring proper apparatus for the schools, grading

General discretionary duties and powers.

and classifying the pupils, and providing separate schools for the different classes in such a manner as will secure the largest attendance of pupils, promote the harmony and advancement of the school, and establishing, when required by the patrons, schools of higher grades of instruction where the advancement and number of pupils require them.

VI. To employ teachers for every school in the county, and to contract with and pay the same for their services; *Provided*, That schools shall not be located nearer than three miles to each other, unless for some local reason or necessity.

[Clause VII repealed by Chapter 4192, June 8, 1893.]

VIII. To audit and pay all accounts due by the Board of Public Instruction.

IX. To keep accurate accounts of all their official acts, proceedings and decisions, of all moneys received, held or disbursed, of all property acquired or disposed of, in a proper set of account books, and a record of the state and condition of each school, and to report the same to the State Superintendent of Public Instruction when required. They shall also at the close of the scholastic year prepare an itemized report of all moneys by them received and disbursed.

X. To prescribe, in consultation with prominent teachers, a course of study for the schools of the county and grade them properly, and to require to be taught in every public school in the county over which they preside, elementary physiology, especially as it relates to the effects of alcoholic stimulants and narcotics, morally, mentally and physically; and all persons applying for certificates to teach shall be examined upon this branch of study, under the same conditions as other branches required by law.

XI. To fix the compensation for the services of the County Superintendent of Public Instruction.

XII. To perform all acts reasonable and necessary for the promotion of the educational interests of the county and the general diffusion of knowledge among the citizens.

XIII. To hold regular meetings for the transaction of business, by arrangement with the State Superintendent of Public Instruction, and to convene a special session on emergencies when requested by the County Superintendent of Public Instruction.

XIV. The Board of Public Instruction in each county shall, on or before the last Monday in June of each year, prepare an itemized estimate showing the amount of money required for

SCHOOL LAWS.

1893.

the maintenance of the necessary common schools in their county for the next ensuing scholastic year, stating the amount in mills on the dollar of the taxable property of the county, which shall not be less than three nor more than five mills, and furnish a copy of the statement to [Board of County Commissioners] and file a copy in the office of the Board of Public Instruction.

[The Board of County Commissioners of the county at a meeting for correcting and reviewing the county assessment shall immediately thereafter ascertain and determine the amount of money to be raised by tax for county purposes....... and shall levy a tax not to exceed five mills nor less than three mills on the dollar on the real and personal property of the county for county school purposes, such tax to be estimated by the County School Board.—Abr. Sec 2, Chap. 4116]. *

XV. To select candidates for admission to the State College and Seminaries.

29. No Board of Public Instruction shall have power to enter into contract with any of its members, except for the purpose of obtaining school sites.

Shall not contract with members. Ib., Sec. 242.

30. It shall be the duty of the County Board of Public Instruction, before every public examination, to appoint a grading committee, and to keep secret the names of persons comprising said committee until its work is performed.

Appoint grading committees. Sec. 14, Chap. 4192, June 8, 1893.

31. It is the duty of the County Boards of Public Instruction in each county to determine the time for the opening of the schools, and to fix within prescribed limits the number of hours that shall comprise a school day.

To fix time for opening schools, and define a school day. Abb., Chaps. 4195 and 4196.

ELECTION OF COUNTY BOARDS OF PUBLIC INSTRUCTION.

32. At the first meeting in July, 1894, the County Board of Public Instruction in each county shall divide their respective counties into three county school board districts so as to place in each district, as nearly as practicable, the same number of qualified voters, the lines of said districts being so drawn as to place each election district wholly within one or another of said county school board districts; and the members of the County School Board [County Board of Public Instruction] shall file in the office of the Clerk of the Circuit Court for such county a certificate of their said action, containing a description of the boundaries of said districts, and naming the election districts comprising each county school board district, which certificate shall be published in a newspaper published in the county, or if there be no newspaper published in the county, then by posting at the county court house door for four weeks thereafter. The County School Board [County

Board of Public Instruction to district county. Sec. 2, Chap. 4193, June 2, 1893.

---

*For the duties of County Commissioners, Assessors, Collectors, Clerks of Circuit Courts and Treasurers in regard to county school fund, see Appendix, Chap. 4115, Secs. 33 and 35.

SCHOOL LAWS.

1893.
When districts may be changed.

Board of Public Instruction] may thereafter change the boundaries of any such districts at a meeting in July of the year of a general election, but such change shall be certified in the clerk's office and published as required for fixing such districts in the first instance.

Term of office. Ib., Sec. 1.

33. That at the next general election (after June 2, 1893), and every two years thereafter, there shall be elected in each county in this State a County Board of Public Instruction, hereinafter mentioned as the County School Board, consisting of three members, whose terms of office shall begin the first Tuesday after the first Monday in January after such election, and terminate upon the qualification of their successors two years thereafter.

Election by County School Board Districts. Ib., Sec. 3.

34. The members of the County School Board [County Board of Public Instruction] shall be elected one from each county school board district by the qualified electors of such district.

Vacancies filled by appointment. Ib., Sec. 4.

35. All vacancies on said board shall be filled for the unexpired term by appointment by the State Board of Education, on the nomination of the State Superintendent of Public Instruction.

Compensation Ib., Sec. 5.

36. The members of the County School Board [County Board of Public Instruction] shall be paid from the county school fund for their services, two dollars per day for each day's service, and not exceeding five cents per mile for traveling expenses. All traveling expenses, before being paid, shall be itemized and approved by the Board.

SCHOOL SUB-DISTRICTS.

What may constitute a School Sub-district. Abbr. Chaps. 4194 and 4197, L. F.

Boundaries defined in petition.

How created.

37. An election may be held under the order and direction of the Board of Public Instruction of any county, if they shall deem it advisable, in any election district [community convenient to any public school, Chapter 4197], or incorporated city or town of such county, upon the petition of one-fourth of the registered and qualified voters thereof, who are tax payers on real or personal property therein, and have paid all taxes due by them for two years next preceding the presentation of such petition, to determine whether such election district [community, Chapter 4197], city or town, shall be a school sub-district; [*Provided*, The petition shall fix and define the boundary of the district or community intended to be made a school sub-district,—Chap. 4197]. Any such election shall be held, and the result ascer-

tained and declared as nearly as practicable in the same manner as is provided by law for the holding of elections concerning Article XIX of the Constitution, substituting the Board of Public Instruction for the County Commissioners. It shall require a majority of the votes of those voting at any such election to determine any matter in the affirmative. If such sub-district is created, three school trustees shall be elected therein, upon a day to be fixed by the Board of Public Instruction, and the same day biennally thereafter.* . Election of Trustees.

38. All voters in such election for sub-districts or trustees shall have the qualifications specified in section 37, for petitioners for elections to establish sub-districts. Qualification of voters.

39. It shall be the duty of these trustees, on or before the last Monday in June of each year, to prepare an itemized estimate, showing the amount of money required for the necessary common school purposes of their sub-district, for the next ensuing scholastic year; stating the rate of millage to be assessed and collected upon the taxable property of their sub-district to cover such amount, not to exceed three mills on the dollar. A copy of the itemized estimate herein provided for shall be filed with the Clerk of the Board of County Commissioners, which Board shall direct the Assessor of Taxes to assess, and the Collector to collect the amount so stated. Moneys collected under provisions of this act shall be paid over to the trustees of the sub-district in which the tax is levied. Duties of Trustees and other officers.

40. These trustees shall, under the direction of the Board of Public Instruction, supervise each school in their district and see that the teachers perform their work promptly and energetically, and that the general work, discipline and morale of the school is satisfactory, and report to the Board of Public Instruction at their regular monthly meetings. Trustees report to County Board of Public Instruction.

41. They shall also be a corporation with the usual powers for the purpose of performing their duties [except that no Board of Trustees shall by contract or otherwise encumber the property of their sub-district—Chapter 4197]. A corporation.

42. They shall receive and hold the money which may be assessed and collected as hereinbefore provided, as a special tax to be disbursed in the district where collected solely for school purposes, such as building school-houses, furnishing the Powers of Trustees.

---

*Both of the acts provide for the election of three trustees biennially; one at the election when the sub-district is created, the other at a subsequent day fixed by the County Board of Public Instruction: not considering this a material difference, the latter has been retained as the law.

18 SCHOOL LAWS.

1893.

Shall give bond.
same, repairing, heating and cleansing, and when necessary paying any legitimate deficit due the teachers. These trustees shall be required to give bond in twice the amount raised by the special tax, to be approved by the County Board of Public Instruction, before receiving any such money.

Sub-district; how abolished
43. Any sub-district may be abolished by like proceedings as those above provided for its establishment.*

> NOTE.—The above will be construed as the law on the subject of sub-districts, until set aside by the courts. Chapters 4197 and 4194, laws of Florida, enacted by the last Legislature, either repeal or re-enact every provision contained in Sections 244 and 245 of the Revised Statutes. These two laws passed by the same Legislature are "*in pari materia*" and must be construed together.

COUNTY SUPERINTENDENT OF PUBLIC INSTRUCTION.

Duties of County Superintendent.
44. The County Superintendent of Public Instruction is directed—

To make inspection. Rev. Stat. Sec. 246.
I. To make timely inspection of the county, to ascertain the location in which schools should be established, the number of youth who would attend each, and the amount of aid that the citizens of the neighborhood will contribute to encourage the establishment of a school.

To visit and examine each school.
II. To visit each school at least once during each school term, and to make a thorough examination of its condition as respects the progress of the pupils in learning, the order and discipline observed, the system of instruction pursued, the attendance of the pupils, the mode of keeping the school records, the character and condition of the school buildings, furniture, books, apparatus and premises, the efficiency of the school supervisor, the interest and co-operation of the citizens in regard to educational matters, and to give such advice as he may judge proper.

To awaken interest in education.
III. To do all in his power to awaken an increased interest in parents, guardians, school supervisors and teachers, with regard to the better education of youth in every respect, and the general diffusion of knowledge.

To confer with Supervisors.
IV. To confer with the school supervisors frequently and see that they attend to their duties, keeping them supplied with a copy of the school laws, decisions, blanks and regulations of the department.

*The latter clause of this section is omitted as a nullity, being at variance with Chapter 4197, which clearly provides that "any community convenient to a public school" may be created a sub-district.

SCHOOL LAWS.   19

> 1893.

V. To select for school supervisors persons whose character, qualifications and sympathy with education specially commend them to those positions. *Concerning selection of Supervisors.*

VI. To keep a record by number, name and description of the locality of each school established, of the expenses incurred for, and of his visits of inspection to, the several schools. *To keep record of each school.*

VII. To notify the State Superintendent of Public Instruction, immediately upon entering his duties, of the names and addresses of all county school officers. *To report names of school officers.*

VIII. To decide upon questions in dispute which arise under the operations of this act, when submitted to him by the parties interested, and to refer his decisions to the Board of Public Instruction. *To decide disputed questions.*

IX. To see that the interests of the county are properly guarded, and its rights secured in the making and performance of every contract for the construction of school buildings, or for other purposes; and that all moneys apportioned to or raised by the county are applied to the objects for which they were granted or raised. *To have general oversight of county school affairs*

X. To examine candidates for teaching and issue certificates in accordance with the provisions of Chapter 4192, Laws of Florida. *To examine candidates and issue certificates. Abbr. Chap. 4192.*

XI. To revoke or suspend certificates, and to suspend those issued by other authority for cause manifestly sufficient, giving notice in writing to the authority issuing them and of the grounds for so doing; also notifying the teacher in like manner, and of the right of appeal, to whom and when such appeal should be made. *To revoke or suspend certificates. Right of appeal. Rev. Stat., Sec. 246.*

45. In case the school supervisor fails to take the census of the children, as * * * * provided in any year when required, then the County Superintendent of Public Instruction shall perform or cause to be performed, that duty, and receive the same emoluments. *When census to be taken by. Abbr., Ib. Sec. 261.*

NOTE.—County Superintendent not authorized to purchase lands for school purposes without being authorized by County Board of Instruction. Board of Public Instruction Nassau County v. Billings, 15 Fla., 686.

SCHOOL SUPERVISORS.

46. Every supervisor is directed—

I. To supervise the work and management of the school and its interests over which he is appointed, and report monthly to the Board of Public Instruction. *To inspect school and report. Rev. Stat., Sec. 247.*

1893.

General duties.

II. To supervise the construction, rental, repair and improvement of the school buildings, furniture, fences, grounds and fixtures; to procure a copy of the school laws, regulations and decisions for the use of the teacher and for his own instruction.

To co-operate with teacher.

III. To attend at all times when requested by, and co-operate with the teacher in his efforts to elevate the character and condition of the school; to review all suspensions from school by the teacher of pupils guilty of gross misconduct and a disregard of and persistent opposition to the authority of the teacher, and to promptly report the same to the County Superintendent of Public Instruction.

To take census. Ib., Sec. 260.

47. It shall be the duty of each school supervisor in the year A. D. 1892 to take the census of all the children over which his supervision extends, between the ages of four and twenty-one and six and twenty-one years, and if any of them be blind or deaf mutes he shall so state, and to report the same on oath to the County Superintendent of Public Instruction on or before the first day of June of said year, and every four years thereafter, for which service he shall receive three cents for each child reported to the County Superintendent;

Penalty for failure.

and upon the failure of the school supervisor to perform this duty he shall be removed from his office.

TEACHERS' CERTIFICATES.

Legal teachers. Sec. 1 Chap. 4192, June 8, 1893.

48. No person shall be permitted to teach in the public schools of this State who does not hold a teachers' certificate, granted in accordance with the provisions of this act.

Grades of Certificates. Ib., Sec. 2.

49. There shall be five grades of certificates issued as herein specified, and named respectively, to-wit: Third Grade, Second Grade, First Grade, State, and Life, Certificate.

Mode of examination. Ib. 3.

50. No certificate, except Life Certificates, shall be issued except on written examination, or written and oral examinations, as provided in this act.

Prerequisites.

51. Any applicant for a certificate of any grade, before being eligible for examination, shall present to the examiner a written endorsement of good moral character from a responsible person, and shall pay an examination fee of one dollar, which fund shall be applied as hereinafter provided.

Fee. Ib. 4.

Qualifications for Third Grade Certificates.

52. An applicant for a Third Grade Certificate shall be examined in orthography, reading, arithmetic, English grammar, composition, penmanship, United States history, geography, physiology, and theory and practice of teaching, and must

make an average grade on the above named branches of sixty (60) per cent., with a grade in no branch below forty (40) per cent. The examination in reading shall be both oral and written. A Third Grade Certificate shall be good for the period of one year from date of issue, and no person shall be permitted to teach longer than one year under a Third Grade Certificate.

1893.

Good for 1 year only. Ib. 5.

53. A Second Grade Certificate shall be issued on examination in the branches as prescribed for a Third Grade Certificate. An average grade of seventy-five (75) per cent. shall be required, with the grade in no branch below fifty (50) per cent., which certificate shall be good two years from date of issue. No teacher shall be granted more than two Second Grade Certificates.

For Second Grade.

Good for 2 years. Ib. 6.

54. An applicant for a First Grade Certificate shall be examined in civil government, book-keeping, algebra, and physical geography, in addition to the branches required for a Third Grade Certificate. An applicant for a First Grade Certificate must make an average grade of eighty (80) per cent., and shall grade in no branch below sixty (60) per cent. A First Grade Certificate shall be good for three years from date of its issue.

For First Grade.

Good for 3 years. Ib. 7.

55. A State Certificate shall be issued only by the State Superintendent of Public Instruction to persons holding a First Grade Certificate and who have taught at least twenty-four (24) months (eight months of which must have been taught in this State successfully under a First Grade Certificate). The Superintendent of Public Instruction shall issue no State Certificate, except on written examination in the following branches in addition to those required for a First Grade Certificate: Geometry, trigonometry, physics, zoology, botany, latin, rhetoric, English literature, mental science and general history. A candidate for a State Certificate must make an average grade on the prescribed branches of eighty-five (85) per cent., with the grade in no branch below sixty (60) per cent. A State Certificate shall be good for five years from date of issue.

State Certificate. By whom issued.

Who eligible.

Qualifications.

Duration. Ib. 8.

56. Any teacher holding a State Certificate issued under this act, and who has taught successfully in a high school in this State for the period of thirty (30) months, may be granted a Life Certificate by the State Superintendent, without further examination, if endorsed by three persons holding State Certificates as possessing eminent teaching ability and as having been eminently successful in governing and conducting a

Life Certificates.

Who entitled to.

SCHOOL LAWS.

1893.

Special Life Certificates. Ib. 9.

school. Nothing in this act shall prevent the State Superintendent from granting Special Life Certificates to eminently successful kindergarten or primary teachers, who have taught three years in this State, good only in that department of schools.

Limit of Certificates. Ib. 16.

57. Third and Second Grade Certificates shall be good only in the county in which they are issued.

First Grade Certificates may be endorsed.

58. Any First Grade Certificate may be endorsed by the County Superintendent of any county in the State, and then will become good for its unexpired time in the county in which it is endorsed as well as in the one in which it was issued.

Extent of State and Life Certificates. Ib. 17.

State and Life Certificates granted in accordance with this act shall be good throughout the State for the periods for which they are granted.

Revocation of Certificates. Ib. 18.

59. A certificate of any grade may be revoked by the authority issuing it, when the holder proves to be unsuccessful, incompetent, or is proven guilty of any gross immorality. A First Grade Certificate may be revoked for any of the above reasons by a County Superintendent endorsing it.

RULES AND REGULATIONS FOR EXAMINATION.

Number and date of examinations. Sec. 19, Chap. 4192, June 8, 1893.

60. There shall be held two examinations a year in each county in the State, beginning on Tuesday after the first Monday in May and September, and each may continue one or more days at the discretion of the examiner and a vote of the examinees; *Provided*, That only one examination may be held in any county, if two be found unnecessary.

Special examinations. Ib. 20.

61. The State Superintendent, for sufficient cause, may order examinations held on days other than those prescribed by Section 19 [60] of this act.

Examination by County Superintendent.

62. Candidates for Third, Second, or First Grade Certificates shall be examined by the County Superintendent of Public Instruction on questions prepared in all cases by the State Superintendent of Public Instruction. The questions shall be sent sealed to the County Superintendents of the various counties, which seal shall not be broken until the morning of the day on which the questions for that day are to be used, and then only in the presence of the persons assembled for examination. Any person or persons who shall be found guilty of securing or attempting to secure the prepared questions, or who shall furnish the prepared questions to any teacher or other person in any other way than prescribed by this act, shall be debarred from teaching a school or from holding any school office in this State. The candidates for certifi-

Seal, when to be broken.

Penalty for cheating in examinations.

cates shall ask no questions, nor receive assistance from any source during the examination. In case any examinee may be in doubt as to the meaning of any question, he or she may state in writing the point in doubt and answer accordingly, which answer shall receive due consideration in grading the papers.

Procedure in case of doubt as to meaning of question. Ib. 10.

63. All examination papers shall be prepared in the presence of the County Superintendent or his appointed assistant, who shall collect the questions and answers on each branch as completed, and said examiner shall accept no paper of any examinee containing a name or mark which would indicate to any other than the examiner its author. Said examiner shall himself, on collecting each paper, designate it by a number known only to himself, and shall keep a record by number and by name of the author of each examination paper. Every examinee shall complete and hand in the answers on each branch before the questions on any other branch shall be given out. When every examinee has completed all the branches, the examiner shall arrange and bundle together all the papers of each examinee and shall deliver the whole to a grading committee.

Procedure in conducting examinations. Ib. 11.

GRADING COMMITTEE.

64. The County Board of Public Instruction, prior to any authorized examination, shall appoint three teachers holding the highest grade certificates among the teachers of the county as a grading committee; said committee shall, immediately after the close of any examination, carefully examine and grade, agreeably to instructions sent out by the State Superintendent, each paper turned over to it by the County Superintendent. When the said committee shall have completed its work, it shall deliver back to the County Superintendent all papers turned over to it with a gradation sheet showing the grade of each examinee in each branch upon which he or she was examined, also the average grade and rank of each examinee. The County Superintendent shall then, for the first time, make known to the grading committee the name corresponding to the number of any examinee, and shall then in the presence of said committee present his list and write on said gradation sheet the name of every examinee after his or her proper number. The said grading committee shall retain one copy of said gradation sheet and shall file one with the County Superintendent, who shall issue certificates to the examinees making averages according to the provisions of Sections 5, 6, and 7 [52, 53 and 54] of this act, and to no others.

Appointment of Grading Committee.

Duties of Committee.

County Superintendent to issue Certificates. Ib., Sec. 12.

SCHOOL LAWS.

1893.

Pay of Grading Committee.

65. It shall be the duty of the County Board to pay the members of the grading committee two dollars a day and 5 cents a mile each way one trip for the actual distance traveled and for the time necessary to perform their work. In esti-

Time allowed.

mating a day, ten hours actual service shall be counted a day, and not more than five days shall be allowed for the completion of the grading of all the papers after any examination.

Balance fund, how applied. Ib. 15.

The grading committee shall be paid out of the fund created by the examination fees and the balance of said fund shall be kept by the County Board and be applied to employing lecturers and to defraying the expenses of Teachers' Institutes in the county.

Examination papers to be filed. Ib. 13.

66. All examination questions and answers prepared by the applicant for certificates shall be filed in the office of the County Superintendent and properly preserved for at least one year; and in case any candidate is dissatisfied with the grading of his or her papers, he or she may authorize the County Superintendent to have his or her answers, with the questions, published in any newspaper the examinee may designate.

PENALTY FOR VIOLATING PROVISIONS OF CHAPTER 4192, RELATING TO HOLDING EXAMINATIONS AND ISSUING CERTIFICATES.

Penalty. Ib., Sec. 21.

67. Any superintendent, county or State, violating the provisions of this act, upon conviction shall be fined not less than fifty nor more than one hundred dollars, and shall be debarred from holding any school office in this State.

DUTIES OF TEACHERS.

68. Every teacher is directed—

With regard to mind and morals. Rev. Strt., Sec. 253.

I. To labor faithfully and earnestly for the advancement of the pupils in their studies, deportment and morals, and to embrace every opportunity to inculcate, by precept and example, the principles of truth, honesty, patriotism, and the practice of every Christian virtue.

Personal habits of pupils.

II. To require the pupils to observe personal cleanliness, neatness, order, promptness and gentility of manners, to avoid vulgarity and profanity, and to cultivate in them habits of industry and economy, a regard for the rights and feelings of others, and their own responsibilities and duties as citizens.

School buildings.

III. To see that the school-house, and all things pertaining thereto, are not unnecessarily defaced or injured.

SCHOOL LAWS. 25

IV. To enforce needful restrictions upon the conduct of the pupils in or near the school house or grounds, avoiding at all times unnecessary severity and measures of punishment that are degrading in their tendency. *1893. To enforce discipline.*

V. To suspend pupils from school for ten days for gross immorality, misconduct or persistent violations of the regulations, giving immediate notice to the parents or guardian of the pupil, and to the school supervisor, of the suspension and the cause of it. *To suspend pupils.*

VI. To hold a public examination at the close of each school term, either oral or written. *To hold examinations.*

VII. To deliver up the keys and all school property to the Supervisor on closing or suspending the school, and in all things to conform to the regulations of the department. *To conform to regulations.*

69. No teacher, while actually engaged in his profession, shall be liable to military or jury duty. *Exemptions. Ib., Sec. 254.*

SCHOOL YEAR, SCHOOL TERM, ETC.

70. Beginning with July 1st, A. D. 1893, the school year for all public schools shall begin on the first day of July and end with the last day of the following June; and all reports, financial and otherwise, to the State Department shall embrace such business and matters only as take place within the limits of the school year thus defined. *Fixing school year. Sec 1, Chap. 4196, June 2, 1893.*

71. The time for the opening of the public schools for each county shall be determined by the County Board of Public Instruction; *Provided*, That all schools must begin so as to close before the last day of June. *Time opening schools. Ib., Sec. 2.*

72. No school in any county shall begin before July first of the school year to which that term of school belongs and for which the apportionment was made. *Not before July 1st. Ib., Sec. 4.*

73. I. A school day shall comprise not less than five (5) and not more than six (6) hours, exclusive of recesses. The time to be fixed by the Board of Public Instruction of each county. *School Day. Chap. 4195, June 6, 1893.*

II. A school month contains twenty days, exclusive of the first and last days of the week. *Month.*

III. A school term contains four school months. *Term.*

IV. The school year contains two terms. *Year.*

1893.

Holidays.
Rev. Stat.,
Sec. 256.

Lost time.
Ib., Sec. 257.

74. All recognized State or national holidays are school holidays.*

75. Lost time may be made up by a teacher at the discretion of the School Supervisor, when no conflict would be occasioned with the arrangements of the Board of Public Instruction.

FORFEITURE OF SCHOOL MONEYS.

When county forfeits.
Rev. Stat.,
Sec. 259.

76. Any county or school district neglecting to establish and maintain such school or schools as the available funds will support, shall forfeit its proportion of the common school fund during such neglect, and in that case all moneys so forfeited shall be apportioned among the several counties at the next annual apportionment.

When a school forfeits.
Sec. 3, Chap.
4196, June 2,
1893.

77. Any public school in the county failing to complete its public term before the terminus of the school year, shall forfeit the proportion of its financial apportionment not used by neglecting or failing to maintain a school for the full term of school in that county, and in that case all moneys so forfeited shall be apportioned among the several schools of the county at the next annual apportionment.

ATTENDANCE FROM ADJOINING COUNTIES.

When permitted.

78. When it is more convenient for youth residing in one county to attend school in an adjoining county, they may do so by the concurrence of the Superintendents of Public Instruction of the two counties. The proportion of school money for each youth shall be transferred by requisition of the County Superintendent of Public Instruction of the county in which the youth resides, upon the Treasurer of the school funds of that county to the Treasurer of the school funds of the county in which the school is located.

Transferring funds.
Rev. Stat.,
Sec. 258.

DUTIES OF CERTAIN OFFICERS.

State Treasurer.
Rev. Stat.,
Sec. 262.

79. The Treasurer of the (State) Board of Education shall keep an account with the several counties, in which he shall credit each county with its proportion of the income of the common school fund, and of the fund raised by the one mill tax authorized by the Constitution, and shall charge each with the amounts receipted for by the Treasurers of the Boards of Public Instruction.

---

*NOTE—The legal holidays are: First day of the week, Sunday; first day of January, New Year's Day; twenty-second day of February, Washington's Birth Day; June third, Birth Day of Jefferson Davis; July fourth, Independence Day; first Monday in September, Labor Day; General Election Day; Thanksgiving Day, and twenty-fifth of December, Christmas Day.—*Vide* Revised Statutes, Section 2315, and Chapters 4058 and 4198, Laws of Florida.

SCHOOL LAWS. 27

80. The several Tax Collectors shall receive only the current funds of the United States in payment for all school taxes; *Provided*, Orders issued by the County Board of Public Instruction shall be receivable in the county where such orders are issued, for county school taxes.

<small>1893.
Tax Collector.
Ib., Sec. 263.
Sec. 40. Chap. 4115.</small>

81. Every officer having moneys which by law go to the State school fund shall pay the same to the State Treasurer, and every officer having moneys which by law go to the county school fund shall pay the same to the County Treasurer.

<small>Other officers.
Ib., Sec. 264.</small>

ARBITRATION.

82. All matters of difference which may arise between school officers and teachers, or other persons, under the operations of this act, shall be submitted to the decision of arbitrators. The proceedings and powers of arbitrators shall be as provided by law for other arbitrations.

<small>Differences may be settled by
Rev. Stat., Sec. 265.</small>

PENALTIES.

83. Whoever imports, prints, publishes, sells or distributes any book, pamphlet, ballad, printed paper or other thing containing obscene language, or any obscene prints, figures, pictures or descriptions manifestly tending to the corruption of the morals of youth, or introduces into any * * * school or place of education, or buys, procures, receives, or has in his possession any such book, pamphlet, ballad, printed paper or other thing, either for the purpose of sale, exhibition, loan or circulation, or with the intent to introduce the same into any * * * school, or place of education, shall be punished by imprisonment in the State prison not exceeding five years, or in the county jail not exceeding one year, or by fine not exceeding one hundred dollars.

<small>Obscene prints and literature.
Rev. Stat., Sec. 2620, Abbr.</small>

84. Whoever willfully cuts, paints, pastes or defaces by writing or in any other manner any school building, furniture, apparatus, appliance, outbuilding, ground, fence, tree, post or other school property, with obscene word, image or device, shall be punished by imprisonment not exceeding fifteen days, or by fine not exceeding one hundred dollars. This section shall not apply to any pupil in and subject to the discipline of the school.

<small>Obscenity on school buildings.
Ib., Sec. 2621.</small>

85. Whoever, within the school-house or grounds, upbraids or insults any teacher in the presence of the pupils, shall be punished by imprisonment not exceeding fifteen days, or by fine not exceeding twenty-five dollars. This section shall not apply to any pupil in and subject to the discipline of the school.

<small>For insulting teacher.
Ib., Sec. 2622.</small>

1893.

For injuring school houses.
Abbr. Sec. 2531, Rev. Stat.

86. Whoever willfully and maliciously, or wantonly and without cause, destroys, defaces, mars or injures * * * * * any school-house, * * * or other building erected or used for the purpose of education or for the general diffusion of knowledge, or any of the outbuildings, fences, walls, or appurtenances of such school-house, * * * or other building, or any furniture, apparatus or other property belonging to or connected with such school-house, * * * or other building, shall be punished by imprisonment not exceeding one year, or by fine not exceeding five hundred dollars.

School officers not to be interested in sale, &c., of text-books.

87. No superintendent or school board of any county, or any person officially connected with the government or direction of the public schools, or teacher thereof, shall receive any private fee, gratuity, donation or compensation, in any manner whatsoever, for promoting the sale or the exchange of any school book, map or chart in any public school, or be an agent for the sale, or the publisher of any school text-book, or be directly or indirectly pecuniarily interested in the introduction of any such text-book; and any such agency or interest shall disqualify any person so acting or interested from holding any school office whatsoever, and shall be deemed a misdemeanor, and upon conviction the party so offending shall be fined in a sum not exceeding fifty dollars, or imprisoned not less than thirty days.

Debarred from holding office.
Rev. Stat., Sec. 266.

Penalty
Ib., 2736.

88. Any superintendent or school board of any county, or any person officially connected with the government or direction of a public school, or teacher thereof, who violates the provisions of Section [87] shall be punished by imprisonment not exceeding thirty days or by fine not exceeding fifty dollars.

Disturbing school.
Abbr. Sec. 629, Rev. Stat.

89. Whoever willfully interrupts or disturbs any school * * * * shall be punished by imprisonment not exceeding thirty days, or by fine not exceeding fifty dollars.

EAST AND WEST FLORIDA SEMINARIES.

Beneficiary scholar.
R.S., Sec 311.

90. Each county in this State east or west of the Suwannee river shall be entitled to send to said seminary in the division in which such county is located, as many scholars or beneficiaries as it may have representatives in the House of Representatives of Florida, who shall receive all the benefits of instruction of said seminary free of all charge.

Board of visitors.

91. At least once in each year each seminary shall be visited by three suitable persons—not members of the board or seminary—to be appointed by the board, who shall examine thoroughly into the affairs of the seminary, and report to the

SCHOOL LAWS.

State Superintendent of Public Instruction their views with regard to its condition, success and usefulness, and any other matters they may judge expedient. Such visitors shall be appointed annually.

92. It shall be the duty of the State Superintendent to visit each seminary at least once in each year, and he shall annually make to the Governor, to be by him laid before the Legislature at each regular session thereof, a full and detailed report of the doings of the respective Boards of Education, and of all their expenditures, and the moneys received for tuition, and the prospects, progress and usefulness of said seminaries, including so much of the report of said visitors as he may deem advisable.

1893.

Shall report to State Superintendent of Public Instruction. Ib., Sec. 312.

State Superintendent shall visit Seminaries.

Shall report. Ib., Sec. 323.

FLORIDA NORMAL SCHOOL AND BUSINESS INSTITUTE.

93. * * * One white student, male or female, from each Senatorial District in the State shall be admitted to all the rights and privileges of the Literary and Classical Departments of the * * * Florida Normal School and Business Institute, free of tuition; *Provided*, That appointments to scholarships to the Florida Normal School and Business Institute shall be made by Senators of the various Senatorial Districts of the State of Florida.

Students admitted free of tuition. Abbr. Sec. 2, Chap. 3869, May 30, 1889.

AGRICULTURAL COLLEGE.

94. Each county shall be entitled to send annually, or so often as vacancies may occur, one student for each member of the Assembly from that county; such student shall be selected by the Boards of Public Instruction of the several counties from among the most advanced pupils in the common and higher schools therein who may present themselves as candidates. Each County Board of Public Instruction shall annually, or as often as vacancies occur which should be filled by the county, give early notice of such vacancy, and of the time and place of meeting for the examination of the candidates. The County Board shall then and there, by themselves, or with the assistance of such persons as they may appoint, examine said candidates, and select those best qualified as to scholastic attainments, good health and upright moral character, and furnish them with certificates of selection for admission, subject to the re-examination and approval of the faculty of the college. In case any Board of Instruction fails to attend to the above duty, then pupils holding high rank in their

Each county entitled to one student for each member of the Assembly.

Selected by the County Board of Public Instruction by examination.

1893.

May make application to the Faculty.
Abbr. Rev. Stat., Sec. 294.

schools in that county may make application in person to the faculty of the college and be examined and admitted on the same terms as they would have been had they passed a preliminary examination before the Board of Instruction of their county. But in case such vacancies remained unfilled, students may be selected from the State at large by the faculty.

Senators shall nominate one student.
Ib., Sec. 295.

95. Each Senator, during his term of office, shall be empowered to nominate one student, who shall be a resident of his Senatorial District, to said State Agricultural College, who shall be entitled to receive the benefit of a full course of instruction at said college without any charge for tuition, subject to such rules and regulations as may be established for the government and direction of said college.

Trustees shall report to Superintendent of Public Instruction.
Ib., Sec 297.

96. The trustees shall make an annual report to the Superintendent of Public Instruction on or before the first day of October, to be by him printed with his report and laid before the Legislature at the beginning of each regular session. Such report shall give a full exposition of the financial condition of the corporation, the progress and improvements made, the nature, cost and results of experiments, and such other matters, including State industrial and economical statistics, as may be supposed useful; one copy of which the Superintendent shall transmit by mail to each of the other colleges which were endowed under the provisions of the act of Congress of July 2, 1862; also a copy to the Secretary of the Interior, and one to each house of Congress.

APPENDIX.

SESSION LAWS OF 1893.

CHAPTER 4192.

AN ACT to Prescribe Rules and Regulations for Licensing Teachers; to Provide for Uniform Examinations; to Secure Fairness in Examinations and in Issuing Teachers' Certificates, and for Other Purposes.

Be it enacted by the Legislature of the State of Florida:

SECTION 1. No person shall be permitted to teach in the public schools of the State who does not hold a teachers' certificate, granted in accordance with the provisions of this Act. *(Who to teach schools.)*

SEC. 2. There shall be five grades of certificates issued as herein specified, and named respectively, to-wit: Third grade, second grade, first grade, State, and life, certificates. *(Certificates, how graded.)*

SEC. 3. No certificate, except life certificates, shall be issued except on written examination, or written and oral examinations, as provided in this Act.

SEC. 4. Any applicant for a certificate of any grade, before being eligible for examination, shall present to the examiner a written endorsement of good moral character from a responsible person, and shall pay an examination fee of one dollar, which fund shall be applied as hereinafter provided. *(Good character.)*

SEC. 5. An applicant for a third grade certificate shall be examined in orthography, reading, arithmetic, English grammar, composition, penmanship, United States history, geography, physiology, and theory and practice of teaching, and must make an average grade on the above named branches of sixty (60) per cent., with a grade in no branch below forty (40) per cent. The examination in reading shall be both oral and written. A third grade certificate shall be good for the period of one year from date of issue, and no person shall be permitted to teach longer than one year under a third grade certificate. *(Qualifications for Third Grade Certificates.)*

1893.

For Second Grade.

SEC. 6. A second grade certificate shall be issued on examination in the branches as prescribed for a third grade certificate. An average grade of seventy-five (75) per cent., shall be required, with the grade in no branch below fifty (50) per cent., which certificate shall be good two years from date of issue. No teacher shall be granted more than two second grade certificates.

For First Grade.

SEC. 7. An applicant for a first grade certificate shall be examined in civil government, book-keeping, algebra, and physical geography, in addition to the branches required for a third grade certificate. An applicant for a first grade certificate must make an average grade of eighty (80) per cent., and shall grade in no branch below sixty (60) per cent. A first grade certificate shall be good for three years from date of its issue.

State Certificates, how issued.

SEC. 8. A State certificate shall be issued only by the State Superintendent of Public Instruction to persons holding a first grade certificate and who have taught at least twenty-four (24) months (eight months of which must have been taught in this State successfully under a first grade certificate). The Superintendent of Public Instruction shall issue no State certificate, except on written examination in the following branches in addition to those required for a first grade certificate : Geometry, trigonometry, physics, zoology, botany, latin, rhetoric, English literature, mental science and general history.

Average Grade

A candidate for State Certificate must make an average grade on the prescribed branches of eighty-five (85) per cent., with the grade in no branch below sixty (60) per cent. A State certificate shall be good for five years from date of issue.

Life Certificates, who entitled to.

SEC. 9. Any teacher holding a State certificate issued under this Act, and who has taught successfully in a high school in this State for the period of thirty (30) months, may be granted a life certificate by the State Superintendent, without further examination, if endorsed by three persons holding State certificates as possessing eminent teaching ability and as having been eminently successful in governing and conducting a school. Nothing in this Act shall prevent the State Superintendent from granting special life certificates to eminently successful kindergarten or primary teachers, who have taught three years in this State, good only in that department of schools.

Mode of examination.

SEC. 10. Candidates for third, second, or first grade certificates shall be examined by the County Superintendent of Public Instruction on questions prepared in all cases by the

State Superintendent of Public Instruction. The questions shall be sent sealed to the County Superintendents of the various counties, which seals shall not be broken until the morning of the day on which the questions for that day are to be used, and then only in the presence of the persons assembled for examination. Any person or persons who shall be found guilty of securing or attempting to secure the prepared questions, or who shall furnish the prepared questions to any teacher or other person in any other way than prescribed by this Act, shall be debarred from teaching a school or from holding any school office in this State. The candidates for certificates shall ask no questions, nor receive assistance from any source during the examination. In case any examinee may be in doubt as to the meaning of any question, he or she may state in writing the point in doubt and answer accordingly, which answer shall receive due consideration in grading the papers.

SEC. 11. All examination papers shall be prepared in the presence of the County Superintendent or his appointed assistant, who shall collect the questions and answers on each branch as completed, and said examiner shall accept no paper of any examinee containing a name or mark which would indicate to any other than the examiner its author. Said examiner shall himself, on collecting each paper, designate it by a number known only to himself, and shall keep a record by number and by name of the author of each examination paper. Every examinee shall complete and hand in the answers on each branch before the questions on any other branch shall be given out. When every examinee has completed all the branches, the examiner shall arrange and bundle together all the papers of each examinee and shall deliver the whole to a grading committee. *Who to prepare examination papers.*

SEC. 12. The County Board of Public Instruction, prior to any authorized examination, shall appoint three teachers holding the highest grade certificates among the teachers of the county as a grading committee; said committee shall, immediately after the close of any examination, carefully examine and grade, agreeably to instructions sent out by the State Superintendent, each paper turned over to it by the County Superintendent. When the said committee shall have completed its work it shall deliver back to the County Superintendent all papers turned over to it with a gradation sheet, showing the grade of each examinee in each branch upon which he or she was examined, also the average grade and *Grading Committee.* *Duties of such Committee.*

SCHOOL LAWS.

1893.

rank of each examinee. The County Superintendent shall then, for the first time, make known to the grading committee the name corresponding to the number of any examinee, and shall then in the presence of said committee present his list and write on said gradation sheet the name of every examinee after his or her proper number. The said grading committee shall retain one copy of said gradation sheet and shall file one with the County Superintendent, who shall issue certificates to the examinees making averages according to the provisions of Sections 5, 6 and 7 of this Act, and to no others.

Where examination papers to be filed.

SEC. 13. All examination questions and answers prepared by the applicant for certificates shall be filed in the office of the County Superintendent and properly preserved for at least one year, and in case any candidate is dissatisfied with the grading of his or her papers, he or she may authorize the County Superintendent to have his or her answers, with the questions, published in any newspaper the examinee may designate.

To keep secret names of Committee.

SEC. 14. It shall be the duty of the County Board of Public Instruction, before every public examination, to appoint a grading committee, and to keep secret the names of persons comprising said committee until its work is performed.

Fees.

SEC. 15. It shall be the duty of the County Board to pay the members of the grading committee two dollars a day and 5 cents a mile each way one trip for the actual distance traveled and for the time necessary to perform their work. In estimating a day, ten hours actual service shall be counted a day, and not more than five days shall be allowed for the completion of the grading of all the papers after any examination. The grading committee shall be paid out of the fund created by the examination fees and the balance of said fund shall be kept by the County Board and be applied to employing lecturers and to defraying the expenses of Teachers' Institutes in the county.

Extent of Certificates.

SEC. 16. Third and second grade certificates shall be good only in the county in which they are issued.

First Grade Certificates to be endorsed.

SEC. 17. Any first grade certificate may be endorsed by the County Superintendent of any county in the State, and then will become good for its unexpired time in the county in which it is endorsed as well as in the one in which it was issued. State and life certificates granted in accordance with

SCHOOL LAWS.   35

1893.

this Act shall be good throughout the State for the periods for which they are granted.

SEC. 18. A certificate of any grade may be revoked by the authority issuing it, when the holder proves to be unsuccessful, incompetent, or is proven guilty of any gross immorality. A first grade certificate may be revoked for any of the above reasons by a County Superintendent endorsing it.

Revocation of Certificate.

SEC. 19. There shall be held two examinations a year in each county in the State, beginning on Tuesday after the first Monday in May and September, and each may continue one or more days at the discretion of the examiner and a vote of the examinees; *Provided*, That only one examination may be held in any county, if two be found unnecessary.

Two examinations.

SEC. 20. The State Superintendent, for sufficient cause, may order examinations held on days other than those prescribed by Section 19 of this Act.

When to be held.

SEC. 21. Any Superintendent, county or State, violating the provisions of this Act, upon conviction shall be fined not less than fifty nor more than one hundred dollars, and shall be debarred from holding any school office in this State.

Penalty.

SEC. 22. All laws and parts of laws in conflict with this Act are hereby repealed.

Repeal.

SEC. 23. This Act shall take effect after January 1st, 1894.

Approved June 8, 1893.

CHAPTER 4193.

AN ACT to Provide for the Election of Members of County Boards of Public Instruction, and to Fix their Compensation.

Be it enacted by the Legislature of the State of Florida:

SECTION 1. That at the next general election, and every two years thereafter, there shall be elected in each county in this State a County Board of Public Instruction, hereinafter mentioned as the County School Board, consisting of three members, whose terms of office shall begin the first Tuesday after the first Monday in January after such election, and terminate upon the qualification of their successors two years thereafter.

Election of County School Boards.

1893.

Duties of County Boards of Public Instruction

SEC. 2. At the first meeting in July, 1894, the County Board of Public Instruction in each county shall divide their respective counties into three county school board districts so as to place in each district, as nearly as practicable, the same number of qualified voters, the lines of said districts being so drawn as to place each election district wholly within one or another of said county school board districts; and the members of the County School Board shall file in the office of the Clerk of the Circuit Court for such county a certificate of their said action, containing a description of the boundaries of said districts, and naming the election districts comprising each county school board district, which certificate shall be published in a newspaper published in the county, or if there be no newspaper published in the county, then by posting at the county court house door for four weeks thereafter. The County School Board may thereafter change the boundaries of any such districts at a meeting in July of the year of a general election, but such change shall be certified in the Clerk's office and published as required for fixing such districts in the first instance.

Boundaries of Districts.

Election by School Districts.

SEC. 3. The members of the County School Board shall be elected one from each county school board district by the qualified electors of such district.

Filling vacancies.

SEC. 4. All vacancies on said Board shall be filled for the unexpired term by appointment by the State Board of Education on the nomination of the State Superintendent of Public Instruction.

Fees.

SEC. 5. The members of the County School Board shall be paid from the county school fund for their services, two dollars per day for each day's service, and not exceeding five cents per mile for traveling expenses. All traveling expenses, before being paid, shall be itemized and approved by the Board.

Repeal.

SEC. 6. All laws and parts of laws in conflict herewith are hereby repealed in so far as they conflict with this Act.

Approved June 2, 1893.

SCHOOL LAWS.   37

CHAPTER 4194.   1893.

AN ACT to Provide for School Sub-Districts in Counties and Towns and to Provide for the Levying and Collection of Taxes for the Support of Schools in such Sub-Districts.

Be it enacted by the Legislature of the State of Florida:

SECTION 1. That an election may be held under the order and direction of the Board of Public Instruction of any county, if they shall deem it advisable, in any election district, or incorporated city or town of such county, upon the petition of one-fourth of the registered and qualified voters thereof, who are taxpayers on real or personal property therein, and have paid all taxes due by them for two years next preceding the presentation of such petition, to determine whether such election district, city or town, shall be a school sub-district. Any such election shall be held, and the result ascertained and declared as nearly as practicable in the same manner as is provided by law for the holding of elections concerning Article XIX of the Constitution, substituting the Board of Public Instruction for the County Commissioners. It shall require a majority of the votes of those voting at any such election to determine any matter in the affirmative. If such sub-district is created, three school trustees shall be elected therein, upon a day to be fixed by the Board of Public Instruction, and on the same day biennially thereafter. *[Election to form School Sub-districts. Mode of election.]*

SEC. 2. All voters in such election for sub-districts or trustees shall have the qualifications specified in section one for petitioners for elections to establish sub-districts. *[Qualifications for voters.]*

SEC. 3. It shall be the duty of these trustees, on or before the last Monday in June of each year, to prepare an itemized estimate, showing the amount of money required for the necessary common school purposes of their sub-district, for the next ensuing scholastic year; stating the rate of millage to be assessed and collected upon the taxable property of their sub-district to cover such amount, not to exceed three mills on the dollar. A copy of the itemized estimate herein provided for shall be filed with the Clerk of the Board of County Commissioners, which Board shall direct the Assessor of Taxes to assess, and the Collector to collect the amount so stated. Moneys collected under provisions of this Act shall be paid over to the trustees of the sub-districts in which the tax is levied. *[Duty of Trustees.]*

SEC. 4. These trustees shall, under the direction of the Board of Public Instruction, supervise each school in their district and see that the teachers perform their work promptly *[Further duties of Trustees.]*

1893.

and energetically, and that the general work, discipline and moral of the school is satisfactory, and report to the Board of Public Instruction at their regular monthly meetings.

To be corporate.
SEC. 5. They shall also be a corporation with the usual powers for the purpose of performing their duties.

Powers.
SEC. 6. They shall receive and hold the money which may be assessed and collected as hereinbefore provided, as a special tax to be disbursed in the district where collected solely for school purposes, such as building school-houses, furnishing the same, repairing, heating and cleansing, and when necessary paying any legitimate deficit due the teachers. These trustees shall be required to give bond in twice the amount raised by the special tax, to be approved by the County Board of Public Instruction, before receiving any such money.

Mode of abolishing.
SEC. 7. Any sub-district may be abolished by like proceedings as those above provided for its establishment. The boundaries of such sub-district shall coincide with the boundaries of the election district, excepting that if a portion an of election district being in an incorporated city or town, shall be included in a sub-district composed of such city or town, the remainder of such election district not included in such city or town, may become a school sub-district in the same manner as though it were an entire election district.

Repeal.
SEC. 8. That all laws and parts of laws in conflict with this Act be and the same are hereby repealed.

SEC. 9. That this Act shall take effect from and after its passage and approval by the Governor.

Approved June 2, 1893.

CHAPTER 4197.

AN ACT to Amend Section 244, and to Repeal Section 245 of Chapter 1, under Title 5, of the Revised Statutes of Florida.

Be it enacted by the Legislature of the State of Florida:

SECTION 1. That Section 244 of Chapter 1, under Title 5, of the Revised Statutes of Florida, be and is amended to read as follows:

Treasurer and his bond.
SECTION 244. ELECTION DISTRICTS OR COMMUNITIES CONVENIENT TO ANY PUBLIC SCHOOL MAY BE FORMED INTO A SCHOOL SUB-DISTRICT.—To determine whether a school sub-district shall be formed, and solely for school purposes, in their

district, the special school tax herein provided for, but may designate one of their number to be treasurer of their board, who shall give a good and sufficient bond and shall pay out the funds of the board only by their order. The trustees shall be a corporation with the powers usual to the same, except that no board of trustees shall by contract or otherwise encumber the property of their school sub-district. The said board of trustees shall be elected biennially, and shall supervise the schools of their districts, and report to the County Board of Education at each meeting, condition of and progress made by the schools of their districts, at least thirty days notice of election held under the provisions of this Act shall first have been given by the County Board of Education, any school sub-district may be abolished in the manner herein provided for its formation.   *Election of Trustees.*

SEC. 2. That Section 245 of Chapter 1, under Title 5, of the Revised Statutes of Florida, be and the same is hereby repealed.

SEC. 3. No previous law shall be construed as opposing the provisions of this Act, election may be held, by order and under direction of the Board of Public Instruction of any county, when on a petition of one-fourth of the registered voters of such district or community who pay real or personal taxes therein, they deem it advisable; *Provided*, The petition shall fix and define the boundary of the district or community intended to be made a sub-school district. At the election held to decide whether such sub-district shall be formed, three school trustees shall be elected, to serve as such, should a majority of the electors, qualified as herein, as and by general statute provided, vote for and create such sub-district. The object of a school sub-district, shall be to promote the school interest of the district or community when formed, by the collection and judicious appropriation of a special school tax, which shall be not less than one, nor more than three mills, at the discretion of the trustees of the sub-district, and the rate fixed by them shall be entered upon the tax roll of the county, and collected by the county Tax Collector, who shall pay the same over to the trustees of the sub-district from whence collected. The trustees shall receive and disburse.   *Manner of election.*   *Petition.*   *Duty of Tax Collector.*

SEC. 4. This act shall take effect on its approval by the Governor.

Approved June 2, 1893.

[NOTE.—This act is printed exactly as enrolled.—Contractor for State Printing.]

1893.

CHAPTER 4195.

AN ACT to Amend Section 255 of the Revised Statutes of the State of Florida, and to Define and Declare what Number of Hours shall comprise a School Day.

Be it enacted by the Legislature of the State of Florida:

SECTION 1. That Section 255, Revised Statutes of the State of Florida, be amended so as to read as follows:

255. SCHOOL DAY, MONTH, TERM AND YEAR.—First. A school day shall comprise not less than five (5) and not more than six (6) hours, exclusive of recesses. The time to be fixed by the Board of Public Instruction of each county. Second. A school month contains twenty days, exclusive of the first and last days of the week. Third. A school term contains four school months. Fourth. A school year contains two terms.

What to constitute a school day.

Approved June 6, 1893.

CHAPTER 4196.

AN ACT to Define a School Year, and to Provide for the Opening and Closing of School Terms.

Be it enacted by the Legislature of the State of Florida:

SECTION 1. That, beginning with July 1st, A. D. 1893, the school year for all public schools shall begin on the first day of July and end with the last day of the following June; and that all reports, financial and otherwise, to the State Department shall embrace such business and matters only as take place within the limits of the school year thus defined.

Beginning of school year.

SEC. 2. The time for the opening of the public schools for each county shall be determined by the County Board of Public Instruction; *Provided*, That all schools must begin so as to close before the last day of June.

Time of opening schools.

SEC. 3. Any public school in the county failing to complete its public term before the terminus of the school year, shall forfeit the proportion of its financial apportionment not used by neglecting or failing to maintain a school for the full term of school in that county, and in that case all moneys so forfeited shall be apportioned among the several schools of the county at the next annual apportionment.

Forfeit of moneys.

SCHOOL LAWS. 41

SEC. 4. No school in any county shall begin before July first of the school year to which that term of school belongs and for which the apportionment is made.

1893.
No school to begin before July 1st.

SEC. 5. All laws and parts of laws in conflict with this Act are hereby repealed.

Approved June 2, 1893.

CHAPTER 4115.
AN ACT for the Assessment and Collection of Revenue.

SEC. 33. The County Commissioners shall determine the amount to be raised for all county purposes, and shall enter upon their minutes the rate to be levied for each fund respectively, and shall ascertain the aggregate rate necessary to cover all such taxes and report the same to the Assessor, who shall carry out the full amount of taxes for all county purposes under one heading in the assessment roll to be provided for that purpose, and the County Commissioners shall notify the Clerk and Auditor of the county, also the Treasurer thereof, of the amount to be apportioned to the different accounts out of the total taxes levied for all purposes, and the County Treasurer in issuing receipts to the Collector shall state in each of his receipts, which shall be in duplicate, the amount apportioned to each fund out of the payment made to him by the Collector, and when any such receipts shall be given to the Collector, by the County Treasurer, he shall immediately file one of the same with the Clerk and Auditor of the county, who shall credit the same to the Collector with the amount thereof, and shall make out and deliver to the Collector a certificate setting forth the payment in detail, as shown by the Treasurer's receipt.

County taxes, rate to be determined.

To be assessed under one heading.

Auditor and Treasurer to be notified.

Duplicate receipts to be issued by Treasurers.

Clerk to issue Certificates.

SEC. 35. As soon as the assessment roll shall be delivered to the Collector, the Clerk of the Circuit Court shall make out and publish a statement showing the amount of taxes charged to the Collector to be collected for the current year, and the apportionment of the same in separate columns to the several funds for which such taxes have been levied, including all poll taxes, and at each monthly meeting of the County Commissioners thereafter, and until the tax books are closed, he shall publish a statement giving each fund credit with the amount collected thereon as shown by the reports of the Tax Collector in his office, and when the tax books are closed he shall publish a like statement showing the amounts specifically allowed

Clerk to publish statement of county taxes separately for each Fund and report collection monthly, also to publish statement when tax books are closed.

When statements are to be posted.

1893.

the Collector on account of errors and insolvencies, and the amount of each fund uncollected. The aforesaid statements shall be posted by the Clerk at the court house door, and published in a newspaper, when one is published in the county, and the costs of publishing the same shall be paid by the County Commissioners. Any Clerk failing to publish such statements, shall be guilty of a misdemeanor, and upon conviction be punished by a fine not exceeding two hundred dollars, or by imprisonment not exceeding one year; and it shall be the duty of the Circuit Court Judges to charge this section to the Grand Juries in their respective circuits.

Penalty.

Duty of Circuit Judges.

RESOLUTION NO. 3.

HOUSE JOINT RESOLUTION Proposing an Amendment to the Constitution of the State of Florida.

Be it resolved by the Legislature of the State of Florida:

That the following amendment to the Constitution of the State of Florida be, and the same is hereby agreed to, and shall be submitted to the electors of the State at the general election in October, A. D. 1894, for ratification or rejection:

Amendment to Sec. 7, Art. XII, of the Constitution.

Section 7, of Article 12, of the Constitution is hereby amended so as to read as follows:

SECTION 7. Provision shall be made by law for the apportionment and distribution of the interest on the State School Fund and all other means provided, including the special tax, for the support and maintenance of public free schools, among the several counties of the State in proportion to the average attendance upon schools in the said counties respectively.

Apportionment of School Fund.

Approved June 2, 1893.

REGULATIONS AND FORMS

PRESCRIBED BY THE

STATE BOARD OF EDUCATION
1893.

DEPARTMENT OF PUBLIC INSTRUCTION,
TALLAHASSEE, DEC. 7, 1893.

In compliance with the provisions of Sec. 21, paragraphs I and VII, the following Regulations, Instructions and Forms have been prescribed by the State Board of Education for the use and guidance of school officers and teachers. (*Vide* Sec. 3, par. I).

REGULATIONS AND INSTRUCTIONS.

GENERAL.

REGULATION 1. Persons to be eligible to offices or positions in this department must possess substantially the following qualifications: Must be of good moral character, temperate, upright, responsible, competent and in full sympathy with the public educational system of the State. *Eligiblity to school office.*

REG. 2. All reasonable rules and regulations prescribed by County Boards of Public Instruction, not at variance with the Statutes or the Regulations and Instructions of the State Board of Education, shall have the full force and effect of law, and must be respected accordingly. *Force of Regulations.*

REG. 3. County school officers and teachers shall in all cases use the blanks, forms, registers, etc., prescribed and furnished by the State Department. *Use of blanks.*

REGULATIONS AND FORMS.

COUNTY BOARDS OF PUBLIC INSTRUCTION.

To be commissioned by State Superintendent.

REG. 4. Members of County Boards of Public Instruction must be commissioned by the State Superintendent of Public Instruction before assuming the duties of the office. As soon as practicable after any general election, the Secretary of State shall deposit with State Superintendent of Public Instruction a certified copy of the election of School Board members in each county, giving name, School Board District and P. O. address of each; and on or before the first day of January thereafter, the State Superintendent shall issue and transmit commissions to said members elect.

To hold regular meetings.

REG. 5. County Boards of Public Instruction shall hold regular meetings, at least monthly during the session of schools, when they shall examine carefully all teachers' reports, issue warrants, hear the report of the County Superintendent and transact other business.

When to issue warrants.

REG. 6. County Boards of Public Instruction shall not issue a warrant to any teacher unless the monthly report of said teacher, on which the warrant is based, is made out in conformity with the blanks furnished, and in compliance with the directions given in the Teacher's Register.

When to contract with teachers.

REG. 7. County Boards of Public Instruction shall not contract with any person to teach a public school who does not hold a Teacher's Certificate granted in accordance with the law, unimpaired by suspension, revocation or limitation. Nor shall any teacher be entitled to compensation from the public school fund for services rendered who has not been employed by, and has not contracted with, said Board.

To assign teachers.

REG. 8. The law makes it the duty of County Boards of Public Instruction to assign teachers and contract with the same, nor are they authorized to delegate this selection either to Supervisors or patrons. But the Supervisor may report to the County Board, for their information in the appointment of teachers, the names of those he thinks best suited to the requirements of the school and most satisfactory to the patrons.

When to assign teachers.

REG. 9. County Boards of Public Instruction shall at the first regular meeting after the May examination in each year, proceed to assign teachers to schools for the ensuing scholastic year, selecting first from the list of county teachers holding State or County Certificates; salaries may be fixed and contracts entered into at a subsequent meeting. After the September examination, all vacancies that may exist or may have occurred shall be filled in like manner.

REGULATIONS AND FORMS.

1893.

REG. 10. The State Board of Education earnestly admonishes County Boards of Public Instruction to exercise great caution in the employment of teachers, that they may not subject themselves to the charge of being unduly influenced by personal favoritism or ties of relationship. *To avoid favoritism.*

REG. 11. The State Board of Education calls the attention of County Boards of Public Instruction especially to the duty of prescribing a uniform course of study for their schools, and grading the same, as provided in Sec. 28, Par. X, of the School Laws;—only a few of the counties having as yet complied with the law in this respect. *To prescribe uniform course of study.*

REG. 12. The State Board of Education recommends to such of the County Boards of Public Instruction as have not already so done, the adoption of a system of rules and regulations for the government of schools, teachers and pupils, and the printing of the same, together with course of study prescribed, in pamphlet form, copies of which should be filed in the office of the State Department. *To print rules and regulations, etc.*

For the guidance of Boards contemplating such action, the State Superintendent shall, upon request, furnish copies of regulations already adopted by other counties.

REG. 13. The State Board of Education recommends to the County Boards of Public Instruction the adoption, for their several counties, of a uniform regulation for the observance of the Christmas holidays, suggesting that all schools suspend not later than December 24th, and resume not earlier than the 2nd day of January following. *Christmas holidays.*

REG. 14. The State Board of Education names the first Friday of February of each year as ARBOR-DAY, which shall *not* be observed as a holiday, but shall be devoted to the planting of trees on school grounds or other appropriate public places, together with suitable exercises, lessons or lectures designed to interest and instruct the children in the care and cultivation of trees. *Arbor Day.*

It is recommended to County Boards to allow no teacher compensation for the day, unless a prescribed number of trees have been properly planted and securely protected against injury. *Teacher's compensation for.*

REG. 15. County Boards of Public Instruction may adopt a regulation requiring pupils from other states, or from other counties than their own, to pay a specified tuition fee to the County Superintendent, to be by him paid to the County Treasurer, and also reported to the Board. *May require tuition fees.*

REGULATIONS AND FORMS.

1893.

To observe 3-mile limit.

REG. 16. The attention of County Boards of Public Instruction is called to the fact that the law expressly prohibits the establishing of schools for the same race nearer than within three miles of each other, unless made necessary by local geographical features.

May combine schools.

Where this law in regard to the locating of schools has been violated in the past, it is now made the duty of the present County Boards of Public Instruction to proceed as speedily as they can consistently with the best interest of all concerned, to correct the same by combining two or more schools when practicable, or by otherwise re-arranging them so as to conform to the provisions of Sec. 28, Par. VI, of the School Laws.

To district counties.

REG. 17. In order that Supervisors and other local school officers may have certain knowledge as to the boundaries of their jurisdiction, and as the law clearly contemplates, it is the duty of the County Boards of Public Instruction to sub-divide their respective counties into permanent local school districts.

To confine attendance to proper district.

The various Boards that have not yet done so, are therefore directed and enjoined to proceed at once, and as speedily as possible, to lay off their respective counties into local school districts, for each race separately, making record of each by name, number, description and boundary, and furnish each Supervisor with a copy of same, together with such regulations as will confine the attendance of pupils within any district to their own district school, except as Boards may provide by regulation; *Provided*, All pupils of the county, qualified therefor, may attend the County High School.

COUNTY SUPERINTENDENT OF PUBLIC INSTRUCTION.

When to make annual report.

REG. 18. The County Superintendent of Public Instruction in each county shall, not later than the fifteenth day of July of each year, prepare and forward to the State Superintendent his Annual Report, in conformity with blanks and instructions sent out from the State Department.

Notice of examinations.

REG. 19. The County Superintendent shall give ample notice before every county examination, of the time and place thereof.

May appoint assistant.

REG. 20. In case separate places are necessary to be provided for the examination of white and negro teachers, the County Superintendent is authorized to appoint a competent assistant to conduct one of the examinations, but he shall be responsible for all the official acts of said assistant.

REGULATIONS AND FORMS.

1893.

REG. 21. County Superintendents are directed to furnish the proper forms, and to see that every applicant for examination files the necessary endorsement of good moral character, as provided in Sec. 51, before admitting such applicant to the examination. *To furnish forms, etc.*

REG. 22. In case a vacancy should exist, or from any cause occur in the teaching force of any school between the regular meetings of the Board, the County Superintendent is authorized to fill the same, subject to the ratification of the Board at its next regular meeting. *When to fill vacancy.*

REG. 23. County Superintendents shall direct teachers to make out all monthly reports for twenty (20) days; should a holiday occur during the month, the teacher should record as the attendance for that day (if not taught) the average attendance for the actual number of days taught during that month. *Teachers' reports.*

SUPERVISORS.

REG. 24. School Supervisors shall be governed in the general discharge of their duties, by the directions and the Rules and Regulations of the County Board of Public Instruction. *How governed.*

REG. 25. The office of Supervisor is not one of control, but of oversight only. Schools while in session are under the immediate control of the County Boards of Public Instruction. But in case of emergency the County Superintendent may suspend or close a school, subject to the action of the Board at its next meeting. *Powers defined.*

REG. 26. The patrons should recommend to the County Superintendent suitable persons for Supervisors (Sec. 28, par. III); but the County Superintendent may exercise some discretion in nominating such to the Board of Public Instruction for appointment (Sec. 44, par. V). *Discretionary power of County Superintendent.*

TEACHERS.

REG. 27. Before beginning a school the teacher must first obtain a certificate, contract with the County Board, procure a register and all necessary blanks. He must keep his register in accordance with the printed directions therein, and must make out his monthly reports in strict conformity to the blanks furnished. *Primary duties of teachers.*

REG. 28. Teachers are notified that there is nothing in the school laws of the State prohibiting the infliction of corporal punishment, when in their judgment it is necessary; *Provided, however,* That such punishment shall not be unnecessarily severe. *Corporal punishment.*

TEACHERS' CERTIFICATES.

Prerequisites for State Certificate.

REG. 29. Applicants for examination for State Certificates, unless personally known to the State Superintendent, must file written evidence of having taught at least twenty-four (24) months under a county First Grade Certificate, or its equivalent, eight (8) months of which time must be shown to have been taught successfully in the schools of this State.

For Life Certificate.

REG. 30. Applicants for Life Certificates must present endorsements in conformity to law, and in accordance with the blanks furnished by the State Superintendent.

For Special Life Certificate.

REG. 31. Applicants for Special Life Certificates must present to the State Superintendent written evidence of having been specially trained for kindergarten or primary work. All such applications must come through County Superintendents, and all applicants must be endorsed by the County Board under which employed, as being eminently successful in that department of school work, and similarly endorsed by all County Superintendents under whom they have taught for the required three years. Blank forms of application will be furnished by the State Superintendent upon application.

Teachers should advance grade of Certificates.

REG. 32. "All teachers should of their own purpose seek from time to time to advance the class of their certificates by diligent and persistent study and the constant reading of the best journals of school work, and books treating of methods, discipline and government of the school, and so pass from the lowest to the highest grade of certificate, and carry with it the increased capacity for the true work of the school room.

"County Superintendents discovering a disposition on the part of certain teachers to remain content with any certificate they may be fortunate enough to obtain, exhibiting no desire to rise higher or to become better qualified for their important work, should at once report the same to the Board of Public Instruction and recommend their removal from the corps of teachers in the county."—Hon. A. J. Russell, Reg. of 1891.

FORMS.

No. 1.

Of Commissions of Members of County Boards of Public Instruction.

DEPARTMENT OF PUBLIC INSTRUCTION, }
STATE OF FLORIDA. }

In the name and by the authority of the State Board of Education:

WHEREAS, ... was duly elected on the ...... day of ...., A. D. 189.., to be the member of the County Board of Public Instruction in and for the county of ...., from the School Board District No...., for the term of two years from the First Tuesday after the First Monday in January, A. D. 189.., and until his successor is elected and qualified according to Chap. 4193, Laws of Florida;

Now, therefore, I, ..., Superintendent of Public Instruction for the State of Florida, under and by the authority vested in me by the laws of the State, and the regulations of the State Board of Education, do hereby commission said .... to be a member of the County Board of Public Instruction of .... county, for the District and term aforesaid, to have, hold and exercise the said office and all the powers appertaining thereto, and to per-

50   FORMS.

form the duties, and receive the privileges and emoluments thereof in accordance with the requirements of law.

In testimony whereof I do hereby set my hand and affix the seal of the State Board of Education, at Tallahas-
[SEAL]   see, the Capital, this the ...... day of ....
A. D. 189..

....
State Supt. Pub. Inst.

No. 2.

Of Appointment of Members of County Boards of Public Instruction.

OFFICE OF THE }
STATE BOARD OF EDUCATION OF FLORIDA, }
TALLAHASSEE, ..., 189.. }

Mr. ....
............, Fla.:

SIR: You are hereby appointed by the State Board of Education of Florida to be a member of the Board of Public Instruction for the county of ...., to fill the unexpired term of ...., ..., member from School Board District No. ...., of county aforesaid.

If accepted, notice of same must be returned on enclosed blank within ten (10) days after receipt of appointment (Sec. 6, Par. I).

Very respectfully,
[SEAL]   ...., Secretary.

No. 3.

Of Acceptance of Appointment of Membership on a County Board of Public Instruction.

............, Fla.,
County of .... 189..

To ....
Secretary State Board of Education:

SIR: I have the honor to accept the appointment by the State Board of Education to be a member of the County Board of Public Instruction for the county of ....

FORMS. 51

from School Board District No. ...of said county, and hereby pledge myself to perform impartially the duties of the office (Sec. 6, Par. 1).

Very respectfully,

....

No. 4.

Of Removing Member of County Board of Public Instruction.

OFFICE OF THE
STATE BOARD OF EDUCATION OF FLORIDA.
TALLAHASSEE,........189..

To............,

........................:

SIR: For [state reason]............you are hereby removed from the County Board of Public Instruction for ....county.

Very respectfully,

................, ...,
Secretary.   Pres. of Board.

No. 5.

Of Recommending School Supervisor.

............, (P. O.) Fla.
............, ..., 189..

To............
Co. Supt. Pub. Instruction:

SIR: Five days notice of the time, place and purpose of the meeting having been given by the Supervisor, the patrons of school No..., at ...., met and organized by the election of the undersigned as Chairman and Secretary.

After ballot of the patrons only, it was found that a majority favored the appointment of Mr. (or Mrs.) ...., of ...., (P. O.) as Supervisor of said school and endorse .... as a citizen of good moral character, temperate, upright, responsible, possessing a fair education, and as one who will perform the duties of the office impartially and faithfully.

................, ...,
Secretary.   Chairman.

No. 6.

Of Appointment of School Supervisor.

OFFICE OF
COUNTY BOARD OF PUBLIC INSTRUCTION
FOR THE COUNTY OF............
............FLA.,........189..

To............,
........................,.

SIR: Having been duly recommended and endorsed as a suitable person to act as Supervisor of school No...., situated at..........., at a meeting of the Board of Public Instruction on the .... day of ...., 189..., you were appointed accordingly (*for four years, or to fill the unexpired term of*), or during the faithful performance of the duties of the office.

Blank form of acceptance herewith enclosed must be signed and returned within ten (10) days, or the appointment will be considered rejected.

Very respectfully,
....
Secretary and County Superintendent.

No. 7.

Of Acceptance of Appointment as School Supervisor.

................, Fla.,
................, 189..

To................,
Sec. and Co. Supt. Pub. Inst.:

SIR: I hereby accept the appointment as School Supervisor for school No...., situated at ...., and pledge myself to perform all the duties of the office faithfully and impartially.

Very respectfully,

FORMS. 53

No. 8.
Of Endorsement of Applicant for County Examination.

..........,........,
..............,....189.

To Co. Supt. Pub. Inst..
.... County:

Sir: This is to certify that I have been personally acquainted with the bearer,..............,for........ years and commend ...... to you as a person of good moral character, and addicted to no habits that could unfit or disqualify ......for the position of teacher.

Very respectfully,
....

No. 9.
Of Application for Examination for State Certificate.

.... Fla.,
.... 189..

To ....,
State Supt. of Pub. Inst.:

Sir: I hereby make application for examination for State Certificate, and enclose herewith testimonials both as to my character and my experience and success as a teacher.

Very respectfully,
....

Applicant must file endorsement from the school authorities under whom he has taught for the last twenty-four months (eight of which must have been in the schools of Florida), and said endorsements must certify to applicant's good moral character and success as a teacher.

No. 10.
Of Recommendation for Life Certificate.

.............., Fla.,
.............., 189..

To ....,
State Supt. of Pub. Inst.:

Sir: We, the undersigned, each of us a holder of a State Certificate granted in accordance with the provisions of Chapter 4192, Laws of Florida, and being well and personally acquainted with the work and character of ...., and having personally observed his methods and noted his success in the class room, both in the matter of instruction and discipline, do therefore endorse .... as a person of eminent teaching ability, and certify that he has been eminently successful in governing and conducting for the past thirty (30) months the High School at ...., in .... county, and commend ...... to you as a teacher worthy and well qualified in every respect to receive a Teacher's Life Certificate.

       Very respectfully,
         ....
          Prin .... School.
         ....
          Prin .... School.
         ....
          Prin .... School.

No. 11.

Of Application for Special Life Certificate.

       OFFICE OF
  COUNTY SUPERINTENDENT OF PUBLIC INSTRUCTION.
    ...., FLA.,........ 189...

To............

   State Superintendent Public Instruction:

SIR: At a meeting of the Board of Public Instruction of .... county, on the.... day of............, 189..., ..., for.... years a teacher in the (*Primary or Kindergarten*) department of the...... graded school of said county, having been nominated by the County Superintendent, was unanimously endorsed by the Board as eminently successful in her department, and is hereby recommended to you as in their judgment well and truly deserving of, and entitled to a Special Life Certificate in that department of school work.

       Very respectfully,
         ....,
................,   Chair. Co. Board Pub. Inst.
Sec. and Supt. Co. Board Pub. Inst.

NOTE—Applicant must file herewith certificate from the Training or Kindergarten school in which she was trained. And if she has not taught the required three years in the above school, this application must be endorsed by all the County Superintendents in the graded schools of whose counties she has taught during the remaining part of the three years.

No. 12.
Of Teacher's Third Grade Certificate.

NOTE.—The different grades of Certificates will be issued in books of 100 each, with stubs. Stubs in all cases must be filled out as indicated.

STATE OF FLORIDA.
No..   [SEAL OF STATE.]   For 1 Year.
TEACHER'S CERTIFICATE—THIRD GRADE.

To the Board of Public Instruction of ....
County:

This certifies that............having presented the requisite endorsement of *good moral character*, and having been legally examined and found to possess the qualifications for *a Third Grade Teacher* as prescribed in Sec. 5, Chap. 4192, an act to provide for the *Uniform Examination of Teachers*, is hereby authorized to contract with your honorable Board, to teach in the public schools of this, ... county within the school year ending June, 30th, 189..

Given under my hand, this....day of...., 189..
.................,
Co. Supt. of Pub. Inst. ....Co.

Standing on examination, scale 100. Orthography .., Reading .., Penmanship .., History .., Arithmetic .., Eng. Grammar ...., Geography .., Composition ....., Physiology .., Theory and Practice of Teaching .., Generel average..

N. B.—No candidate can be awarded this certificate who fails to make a generel average of 60 per cent., or falls in any branch below 40 per cent.

Form of Stub to Third Grade Certificate.

No... Date of issue....., 189.., To...., Sex...., Race...., Age.., Home P. O. ...., Certificate expires.........
Standing on examination same as in body of certificate.

No. 13.

Of Teacher's Second Grade Certificate.

STATE OF FLORIDA.

No..   [SEAL OF STATE.]   For 2 Years.

TEACHER'S CERTIFICATE—SECOND GRADE.

To the Board of Public Instruction .. .. county:

This certifies that .... having presented the requisite endorsement of *good moral character*, and having been legally examined and found to possess the qualifications for a *Second Grade Teacher* as prescribed in Sec. 6, Chap. 4192, an act to provide for *Uniform Examination of Teachers*, is hereby authorized to contract with your Honorable Board, to teach in the public schools of this .... county, for the school years ending June 30th, 189.., and June 30th, 189..

Given under my hand, this the .. day of ...., 189..

.................,
Co. Supt. of Pub. Inst.

Standing on examination. (Subjects same as for Third Grade.)

N. B.—No candidate can be awarded this certificate who fails to make a general average of 75 per cent., or falls in any branch below 50 per cent.

Form of Stub for Second Grade Certificate.

No.., Date of issue.....189.., To....., Sex...., Race...., Age.., Home P. O........, Has taught ... months, Last Certificate was....Grade, Issued from ...... county, Dated ...., Standing on examination same as in body of certificate.

No. 14.

Of Teacher's First Grade Certificate.

STATE OF FLORIDA.

No..   [SEAL OF STATE.]   For Three Years.

TEACHER'S CERTIFICATE—FIRST GRADE.

To County Boards of Public Instruction, Greeting:

Be it known that .... having presented the requisite endorsement of *good moral character*, and having passed satisfactory examination as prescribed in Sec. 7, Chap. 4192, an act to provide for the *Uniform Examination of Teachers*, is therefore entitled to the rank of *First Grade Teacher*, and is hereby licensed to teach in the Public Schools of .... county for the term of three years from date.

Given under my hand this the .... day of ...., 189...

....
Co. Supt. of Pub. Inst.

Standing on examination, scale of 100. Orthography ..; Reading .., Penmanship .., U. S. History .., Geography .., Eng. Grammar .., Arithmetic .., Composition ...., Physiology .., Theory and Practice of Teaching .., Civil Government .., Book Keeping .., Algebra .., Physical Geography .., General Average ..

N. B.—This certificate may be endorsed upon the reverse side by any County Superintendent; and so endorsed becomes good for its unexpired term in such county. *Vide* Sec. 17, Chap. 4192.

(The following will be contained in side stub to this certificate.)

No.·., Issued...., 189.., To...., Sex...., Race...., Age .., Home P. O...., No months taught..,Grade of last Certificate...., Where issued, ... Date of same...., (Standing on Examination same as in body of certificate).

No. 15.
Of Teacher's State Certificate.

STATE OF FLORIDA.
No.. [SEAL OF STATE.] For Five Years
TEACHER'S STATE CERTIFICATE.

OFFICE OF }
SUPERINTENDENT OF PUBLIC INSTRUCTION, }
TALLAHASSEE, ..., 189.. }

To County Boards of Public Instruction:

Whereas, The bearer .... has presented evidence to show that ... has taught successfully at least twenty-four months (eight or more of which in schools of Florida), and that .... is a person of good moral character, possessing ability to govern and aptness to teach, and has passed satisfactory examination in the branches prescribed in Sec. 8, Chap. 4192, an

58 FORMS.

act to provide for the *Uniform Examination of Teachers* ... is hereby licensed to teach in any county in this State, and exempt from further examination for five years from date.

Witness my hand and the Seal of the State Board of Education, this the .... day of ...., 189..

....
State Supt. of Pub. Inst.

Standing on Examination—

Spelling....	Reading....	Writing....	Arithmetic..
Grammar...	Composition.	U. S. History	Geography...
Pedagogics.	Physiology..	Civil Gov...	Book keeping.
Algebra....	Phys. Geog..	Geometry...	Trigonometry.
Physics....	Zoology.....	Botany....	Latin.......
Rhetoric...	Eng. Lit.....	Ment. Sci...	Gen. History.
Average....			

No. 16.

Of Teacher's Life Certificate.

STATE OF FLORIDA.

TEACHER'S LIFE [SEAL OF STATE.] CERTIFICATE.

Alios Docendo Discimus.

The eminent qualifications of .... as a teacher of youth, having been shown by .... distinguished success in the schools of this State, and having presented the requisite endorsements and testimonials as provided by Sec. 9, Chap. 4192, Laws of Florida, ... is therefore awarded this Diploma which is of perpetual validity, and forever exempts .... from further examination as a teacher in the public schools of this State.

Given under my hand and the Seal of the State Board of Education, at the city of Tallahassee, this the... day of.....189..

................,
State Supt. Pub. Inst.

No. 17.
Of Primary Life Certificate.
STATE OF FLORIDA.

PRIMARY LIFE   [SEAL OF STATE.]   CERTIFCATE.

OFFICE OF }
SUPERINTENDENT OF PUBLIC INSTRUCTION. }
TALLAHASSEE, ... 189.. }

WHEREAS, The bearer............has been recommended by the County Superintendent of Public Instruction of............county, and has presented the requisite endorsements and filed the necessary evidence to show that.... has been especially trained for Kindergarten or Primary work, and by three years' successful teaching in this State has demonstrated..... *Eminent Qualifications* as a primary teacher;

Therefore, By authority reserved to me in Sec. 9, Chap. 4192, Laws of Florida, I have this day awarded............ this Certificate, which is of perpetual validity, and secures to ....the privilege of teaching, without further examination, in the Primary Department *only* of any regularly graded school in the State of Florida.

Witness my hand and the Seal of the State Board of Education, this the.... day of ...... 189...

................,
State Supt. of Pub. Inst.

No. 18.
Of Suspension or Revocation of a Teacher's Certificate.

OFFICE OF THE }
BOARD OF PUBLIC INSTRUCTION, }
FOR....COUNTY....189.. }

To............,
........, Fla.:

DEAR....: It is my unpleasant duty to inform you that certain charges have been preferred against you, on apparently sufficient grounds, alleging that (state the charges plainly and briefly—see Section 44, Par. XI), in consequence of which your certificate to teach a public school is hereby declared suspended (or revoked, as the case may be), and the right to teach a public school in this State, as well as the privileges conferred by said certificates, are suspended (or revoked, as the case may require), until further notice.

The case will be presented to the Board of Public Instruction (or Superintendent of Public instruction, if the certificate had been issued by him; also, state the time and place at which a hearing will be granted), at which time you shall have an opportunity to make a full and fair vindication of the charges, in conformity to the regulations of the Department of Public Instruction.

Very respectfully,

....
Co. Supt. of Pub. Inst.

No. 19.

Of Contract with Teacher.

This contract, by and between........, a legally licensed Teacher, and the Board of Public Instruction for the county of........, State of Florida, witnesseth: That the said.... agrees to teach (as principal, 1st or 2nd assistant, as the case may be), in the Public School No..., at ......, or such other Public School as the Board may elect, commencing on the ... day of ......, 189.., for the term of....months, and to perform well and faithfully the duties of Teacher according to law and the Regulations of the Department of Public Instruction of Florida and the Rules and Regulations of the Board of Public Instruction of...... county. The Board on its part reserves the right to change the salary specified in this contract; to shorten or lengthen the term specified herein; or, for sufficient cause, to annul the contract altogether, as the success or failure of the Teacher seems to justify, or as..... conforms or fails to conform to the Rules and Regulations of this Board.

For and in consideration of services rendered, the said Board of Public Instruction of......county, agrees to pay to the said...... the sum of......Dollars per school month, and to give such other aid as the law requires.

Signed:

....
Teacher.

....
Sec. and Co. Supt.

By order and on behalf of County Board of Public Instruction.

Witnesses:
....
....

N. B.—The original must be filed in the office of the County Superintendent, who may give any teacher a duplicate on demand.

No. 20.

Of Award of Board of Public Instruction on Charges Against a Teacher on Appeal.

OFFICE OF
THE BOARD OF PUBLIC INSTRUCTION
FOR THE COUNTY OF...., ..., 189..

To............,
    Teacher:

After a fair and careful examination, on appeal, of the charges preferred against you by ...., to-wit: ..... (recite the charges plainly and briefly,) it appears to this Board that .... (state the conclusion of the Board) you are hereby honorably acquitted and continued in your position in .... (or censured and discharged from, as the case may be) the service of this Board. Your salary will be continued from the time of your suspension, ... (or will not be continued, in case the suspension is confirmed or certificate revoked.)

                          ...., Chairman.

................,
    Sec. and Co. Supt. of Pub.-Inst.

No. 21.

Of Notice of Suspension of Pupil by a Teacher.

SCHOOL No. ...., 189..

To............,
    School Supervisor:

I regret to be compelled to inform you that under the provision of the school law (Section 68, Par. V), I have found it necessary, for the good of the school, to suspend..........

(name pupil) from attendance at school for .... (not exceeding ten) days. The cause for such suspension is .... Have the kindness to call on me at your earliest convenience, to extend such aid and advice, and take such further action as you may judge proper, according to Section 46, Par. III. of the law.

Very respectfully,
................, Teacher.

NOTE.—The teacher must also give immediate notice to the parents or guardian of the pupil, (Sec. 68, Par. V). This may be done by modifying the above form, but is always best done in person.

At the interview, the teacher should carefully avoid finding needless fault with the child, and should manifest such kindly spirit toward both parent and child as should satisfy them that the suspension was not prompted by any malice, but only for the reformation of the pupil and the good of the school.

Indeed, a frank interview with the parent or guardian in advance of suspension would often render a resort to such a measure unnecessary.

In all cases of suspension, the teacher must report the matter, with the facts, both to the Supervisor and parents. The Supervisor must review all suspensions and report the same promptly to the County Superintendent, (Sec. 46, Par. III), whose action on the matter shall be final.

No. 22.

Of Notice for Called Meeting of Board.

OFFICE OF
BOARD OF PUBLIC INSTRUCTION,
FOR....COUNTY......189..

To................,
   Member Co. Bd. of Pub. Inst.:

SIR: I have the honor to request your attendance at a special meeting of the County Board of Public Instruction, to be held at......, on the....day of......, at the hour of ....(a. m. or p. m), for the purpose of......(state the object of the meeting).

....
Sec. and Co. Supt. of Pub. Inst.

FORMS.

No. 23.

Of Warrant on a Treasurer of County Board of Public Instruction.

STATE OF FLORIDA.

No... To the Treasurer of.... County Board of Public Instruction.

Pay to the order of...................................
.... Dollars
[Seal of the State.]
From any money belonging to the County School Fund, for services as teacher in school No...at............. Given at ...., Fla, this .... day of ....189...
$....,
Countersigned by
....
Sec. and Co. Supt. Pub. Inst.   Chair. Co. Board Pub. Inst.

Form of Stub.

School Warrant. No..... $.... Issued...........,189..
To............, Teacher of school No...at..............
Payable out of County School Fund. For salary ....
month. Received by me..............

No. 24.

Of Notifying Comptroller Who is Authorized to Receive County School Fund.

Office of
Board of Public Instruction, for the
County of...., ..., 189..

To Hon..........., Comptroller,
Tallahasssee, Fla.:

Sir: This is to certify that....... is Treasurer of....... county, and is authorized to receive the sum apportioned to said county from the interest of the State School Fund (or one-mill tax) for the year 189..

....
Chair. Co. Bd. of Pub. Inst.

....
Co. Supt. of Pub. Inst.

No. 25.

Of Requisition on the Comptroller for School Fund.

                                 OFFICE OF
           BOARD OF PUBLIC INSTRUCTION FOR THE
               COUNTY OF............,........189..

To Hon............:......, Comptroller,
                Tallahassee, Fla.:

SIR: We hereby make application for $...., the sum apportioned to .... county from the interest on the State School Fund (or one,mill tax) for the year 189..

                               ....
                       Treasurer of .... County.

....
Chair. Co. Bd. Pub. Inst.

No. 26.

Of Bond of Trustees of School Sub-District. Sec. 6, Par. II, and Sec. 42.

Know all men by these presents, That we; A B, C D, and E F. Trustees of School Sub-District No. ... county of........, State of Florida as principals, and G H and J K, their sureties, are held and firmly bound unto the Board of Public Instruction of said county in the sum of (insert double the amount that will be liable to fall into their hands at any time) for the payment of which sum well and truly to be made, we firmly bind ourselves, our heirs, executors and administrators, jointly and severally, by these presents.

The condition of this obligation is such, that if the said A B, C D and E F, Trustees of School Sub-District No..., county and State aforesaid, shall faithfully appropriate to their proper and lawful uses, as provided in section 43 of the school laws, all moneys or other property that may come into their hands by virtue of their office, and render promptly the required returns, and turn over to their successors all bonds, records and effects, then this obligation shall be void, otherwise of full force and virtue.

                                     A B Seal.
                                     C D Seal.
                                     E F Seal.
                                     G H Seal.
                                     I K Seal.

No. 27.

Of Contract for Building a School House.

STATE OF FLORIDA }
..........COUNTY. } This contract made and entered into between A B of the county of........, State of Florida, and the Board of Public Instruction for the county of........, State of Florida, and their successors in office.

In consideration of the sum of one dollar in hand paid to A B, the receipt whereof is hereby acknowledged, and of the further sum of.... (insert total amount) to be paid as hereinafter provided, the said A B agrees to build a........ (describe the building here merely in general terms as log, frame, brick, etc.,) and to furnish the material therefor, according to the plan and specifications for the construction of said house, hereunto appended, at........ (describe the locality) and on such lot as the Board my direct.

The said house is to be built of the best material, in a substantial, workmanlike manner, and is to be completed and delivered to the said Board, or their successors in office, free from any lien for work done or material furnished, by the ......day of......, 189..; and in case the house is not finished and ready for delivery by the time herein specified, the said A B shall forfeit and pay to the said Board, or their successors in office, for the use of the public schools of the county, the liquidated sum of......, (insert the forfeit money) and shall also be liable for all damages that may result to said Board in consequence of such failure.

The said Board hereby agrees for themselves, and their successors in office, to pay the said A B the sum of..... dollars when the said house is finished and delivered as herein stipulated (or, as is usual in costly buildings, the Board may pay in installments as the work progresses, as follows: The sum of ....dollars when the foundation of the house is finished; and the further sum of.... dollars when the walls are up to the square and ready for the roof, the remaining sum of....dollars when the said house is finished, etc.).

It is further agreed that this contract shall not be sub-let, transferred or assigned, without the mutual consent of both parties.

Witness our hands and seals this.....day of...... A. D. 189..

       A B,
       ....
         Contractor.
      ....
     Chair. Co. Bd. of Pub. Inst.
      ....
     Sec. and Co. Supt. Pub. Inst.

Witnesses:
....
....

NOTE.—Plans and specifications should be attached to the contract.

A Board should not attempt to build a permanent and expensive school-house without first getting some good mechanic or architect to draw up full and distinct plans and specifications.

No. 28.
Of Deed by Husband and Wife.

NOTE.—It is the duty of County Boards of Public Instruction to endeavor to get titles *in fee simple* to all school property (Sec. 28, Par. I). The following form will answer in either case, whether the wife owns the property, or only signs to release dower.

STATE OF FLORIDA, }
.... County. } Know all men by these presents, That we, A B and C D, his wife, of the county of ......, State of Florida, in consideration of the sum of ...... dollars to us in hand paid, and by us received, do hereby bargain, sell, grant and convey unto the Board of Public Instruction for the county of......, State of Florida, and their successors in office, the following described premises, situated in the county and state aforesaid, to-wit: (Describe definitely the premises by giving starting point, metes and bounds), together with all the tenements, hereditaments and appurtenances thereto belonging or in anywise appertaining; to have and to hold in fee simple forever.

In witness whereof the said A B, as well as C D, his wife, who joins in this conveyance for the purpose of absolutely transferring all of her claims to, and relinquishing and conveying all of her estate and her right of dower in the above described premises, have hereunto set their hands and affixed their seals, this .... day of ...., in the year one thousand eight hundred and ninety-..... .

A B, (SEAL)
C D. (SEAL)

Signed, sealed and delivered
in presence of us—
....
....

STATE OF FLORIDA, }
.........COUNTY. } I,............:....a................
(*Justice of the Peace*, or *Notary Public as the case may be*) in and for the State and county aforesaid, do hereby certify that on this....day of........A. D. 189.. in said county, before me in person appeared *A B* and *C D*, his wife, and both of them to me personally known, each of whom did duly and severally say and acknowledge before me that they and each of them did execute, sign, seal and deliver the foregoing deed of conveyance for the uses and purposes therein expressed. And the said Mrs. *C D* ......, upon an examination had and made by me separately and apart from her said husband, did say and acknowledge before me that she executed, signed and sealed said deed for the purpose of absolutely conveying, releasing, relinquishing and renouncing all of her estate, right, title and interest in and to the land in said deed described, whether the same be a dower interest or estate, or an independent separate estate in her own right, and that she did the same freely and voluntarily and without any compulsion, constraint, apprehension or fear of or from her said husband.

In witness whereof I hereunto, in the presence of the said acknowledgers, set my hand and seal the...day and year above written.

A B..........(sign here.)
C D... ......(sign here.)

................[SEAL.]
(J. P. or Notary sign here and attach private or official seal.)

No. 29.

Of Itemized Estimate.

OFFICE OF
THE BOARD OF PUBLIC INSTRUCTION
FOR...... COUNTY, JUNE...., 189..

To Hon............, *Chairman, and Members of the Board of County Commissioners:*

SIRS—The County Board of Public Instruction in session on this day found the following funds necessary for school operations in...... county for the school year beginning July 1st, A. D. 189.. and ending June 30th, A. D. 189..

For payment of outstanding warrants............ $ ——
For purchase of text-books, charts, etc............ ——
For construction of school-houses............... ——
For rent of school-houses...................... ——
For repair of school-houses.................... ——
For insurance of school-houses................. ——
For incidental expenses of schools.............. ——
For furniture for schools...................... ——
For per diem and mileage of School Board...... ——
For incidental expenses of Board and Co. Supt.... ——
For salary of County Superintendent of Schools... ——
For salary of teacher of school No. 1 for..... Mos. ——
For salary of teacher of school No. 2 for .... Mos. ——
For salary of teacher of school No. 3 for..... Mos. ——

(Complete the list of schools.)

Total .... $ ——

We believe that a levy of... mills on the taxable property of the county will be necessary to give us the amount we imperatively need, and we hereby request you to levy the same in accordance with Sec. 2, Chapter 4116 Laws of Florida.

By order of the County Board of Public Instruction.

....,
Chair. Co. Board of Pub. Inst.

. ...,
Sec. and Co. Supt. of Pub. Inst.

INDEX.

A.

Pye. Sec. Par.

ACTS OF LEGISLATURE 1893—
   See LAWS, SESSION OF 1893.
ACCOUNTS—
   Audited and paid by Co. Board of Pub. Inst..... 14 28 VIII
AGRICULTURAL COLLEGE—
   Beneficiaries of................................ 29 94
   Vacancies in county's quota, how filled........ 29 94
   When application may be made direct.......... 29 94
   Senators may nominate pupils................. 30 95
   Trustees must report to State Supt............ 30 96
APPOINTEES—
   Must notify of acceptance.................... 8 6 I
   Certain pledge required of .... 8 6 I
APPEALS—
   State Supt. may decide on or refer............ 11 21 VI
   State Board to decide, when referred to them.... 9 8 III
   Mode of making, prescribed by State Board...... 9 8 III
APPENDIX.. 31
ARBOR-DAY—
   Regulations concerning....................... 45 14
ARBITRATION—
   Disputes settled by, procedure................ 27 82
ATTENDANCE—
   From adjoining counties...................... 26 78
   From other schools in same county............ 46 17
   How recorded for holidays not taught......... 47 23

APPARATUS—
 County Board to provide........................ 13 28 V
 Penalty for defacing....................... 27 84
APPLICANTS—
 For examination requirements of............... 20 51

B.

BOARD OF MANAGERS—
 Of Institute for Blind, Deaf and Dumb. State
  Board to be............................. 10 12
 General duties of............................. 10 14
 Shall provide necessary clothing, etc, for inmates 10 17
 Shall provide for education of inmates......... 10 18
 Shall report to Legislature.................... 11 19
 See also INSTITUTE FOR BLIND, DEAF AND DUMB.

BOARD OF COUNTY COMMISSIONERS—
 See COUNTY COMMISSIONERS.

BOARD OF EDUCATION—
 See STATE BOARD OF

BOARD OF PUBLIC INSTRUCTION—
 Consists of three members.................... 16 33
 Elected biennially............................ 16 33
 One from each School Board District.......... 16 34
 When term of office begin..................... 16 33
 Vacancies on, how filled...................... 16 35
 Compensation of members..................... 16 36
 See also..................................... 13 25
 How commissioned............................ 44 4
 Special regulation concerning election of...... 15 32–34
 To be a corporation, powers defined........... 12 22
 Procedure of organization.................... 12 23
 Hold titles to county school property.......... 13 24
 Do not control School Sub-Dist. property...... 13 24
 Co. Supt. to be Secretary of.................. 13 26
 Co. Treasurer, Treasurer of................... 13 27
 Duties of..................................... 13 28
 To hold and manage Co. school property...... 13 28 I

BOARD OF PUBLIC INSTRUCTION—(Continued.)

To locate and maintain schools	13	28	II
To appoint Supervisors	13	28	III
To select school sites	13	28	IV
To establish High schools	13	28	V
To employ, contract with, and pay teachers	14	28	VI
To audit and pay accounts	14	28	VIII
To keep record of official acts	14	28	IX
To make certain reports	14	28	IX
To grade schools and prescribe courses of study	14	28	X
To fix compensation of Co. Supt	14	28	XI
Plenary powers	14	28	XII
To hold regular meetings	14	28	XIII
May be convened by Co. Supt	14	28	XIII
Shall prepare itemized estimate sheet	14	18	XIV
Select candidates for admission to State Colleges and Seminaries	15	28	XV
May not contract with members, except	15	29	
To appoint grading committee	15	30	
To fix time of opening schools, etc.	15	31	
Shall hold monthly meetings, at least	44	5	
May refuse to issue Teacher's warrants, if	44	6	
With whom may contract to teach	44	7	
Who entitled to compensation from, as teacher	44	7	
Must assign and contract with Teachers	44	8	
May not delegate this duty	44	8	
When shall assign teachers to county schools	44	9	
Caution in employment of teachers	45	10	
To prescribe course of study, etc	45	11	
To adopt and print rules and regulations	45	12	
Recommendation concerning Christmas holidays	45	13	
May charge tuition of non resident pupils	45	15	
Must observe the "3-mile limit"	46	16	
To sub-divide county into permanent School Districts (q. v.)	46	17	

See also SCHOOL BOARD DISTRICTS.

BLANKS—
  Printing and distribution of................ 11 21   I
  Use of by Co. Supt 46 18
  Use of by Teacher......................... 47 27
BOND—
  When required and by whom fixed............. 8 6   II
  Trustees of sub-district must give 18 42
BUILDINGS, SCHOOL—
  Duty of Board to provide and care for .... 13 28   V
  Penalty for defacing.......................... 28 86

C.

CENSUS of School Population—
  Supervisor to take every four years............ 20 47
  Regulation concerning........................ 20 41
  When Co. Supt. may take 19 45
CERTIFICATES OF LICENSE TO TEACH IN PUB.
  SCHOOLS—
    General provisions concerning............... 20 48–59
    A prerequisite to teaching.................... 20 48
    Grades of 20 49
    How issued 20 50
    Examination for. See EXAMINATION.
    By whom may be revoked.................... 22 59
    Form of revocation........................... 59
    Applicant for must file endorsement........... 20 51
    Form of endorsement........................ 53
    Provisions concerning Third Grade............. 20 52
    Form of Third Grade......................... 55
    Provisions concerning Second Grade 21 53
    Form of Second Grade 56
    Provisions concerning First Grade 21 54
    Form of First Grade 56
    Second and Third Grade good only in county issu-
      ing 22 57
    First Grade may be endorsed in other counties... 22 58
    By whom First Grade may be revoked.......... 22 59
    See also "EXAMINATION."

CERTIFICATE. STATE—
   See STATE CERTIFICATE.
CERTIFICATE, LIFE—
   See LIFE CERTIFICATE.
CERTIFICATE, SPECIAL LIFE—
   See PRIMARY LIFE CERTIFICATE.
COUNTY COMMISSIONERS—
   Issue certificate of admittance to Institute for Blind,
     Deaf and Dumb 10 15
   Supply means of transportation 10 16
   Shall levy school tax estimated by School Board. 15 28 XIV
   Shall levy special tax estimated by trustees sub-
     districts 17 39
COUNTY BOARD OF PUBLIC INSTRUCTION—
   See BOARD OF PUBLIC INSTRUCTION.
CONVENTION OF SCHOOL OFFICERS—
   For what and by whom may be called............. 11 21 II
CONTRACT—
   Form of for building school house............... 65
   Form of teachers'................................... 60
COUNTY SCHOOL FUND—
   All moneys going to must be paid to County Treas-
     urer... 27 81
COURSE OF STUDY—
   In each county must be prescribed by Co. Board. 14 28 10
   Should be published............................. 45 12
**COUNTY SUPERINTENDENT OF PUBLIC IN-
STRUCTION.**
   Is Sec. of Co. Bd. of Pub. Inst.................. 13 26
   Compensation of .... 14 28 XI
   May call special meetings of Board............. 14 28 XIII
   Duties of... 18 44
   When required to keep schools .... 18 44 I
     to visit schools............................... 18 44 II
   With regard to awakening educational interest.. 18 44 III
   With regard to supervisors .... 18 44 IV-V
   With regard to keeping record of schools........ 19 44 VI

COUNTY SUPERINTENDENT OF PUBLIC IN-
STRUCTION—(Continued.)

    With regard to State Supt. Pub. Inst... .... 19 44 VII
    To decide disputes, or refer to Board. .... 19 44 VIII
    To protect the educational interests of Co....... 19 44 IX
    To examine applicants and issue 1st, 2nd and 3rd
        grade certificates....................... ...... 19 44 X
    May revoke certain certificates for cause .. .... 19 44 XI
    When may take census 19 45
    Not authorized to purchase land for Board...... 19 45 Note
    Shall make annual report to State Supt 46 18
    Shall give notice of examinations....... .... 46 19
    May appoint an assistant examiner........ ...... 56 20
    Shall require applicants for examination to file en-
        dorsements.... .... 47 21
    When may appoint a teacher................... 47 22
    Allowed discretion in nominating supervisors.... 47 26

D.

DAY—
    See SCHOOL DAY.

DEPARTMENT OF PUBLIC INSTRUCTION—
    Officers of...................................... 7 2
    State Supt. to prescribe rules and regulation for. 11 21 VII
    Officers shall conform to regulations of..... .... 7 3 I
    Tenure of office in .... 7 3 II

DISTRICT—
    Permanent school.
    Counties to be sub-divided into.... .... 46 17

DISPUTES—
    Arising under school laws
    Co. Supt. to decide or refer to Board .. .. 19 44 VIII

DEED—To school grounds.
    Form of. 66

E.

EDUCATION, HIGHER—
    State Board of Education to foster .... 9 8 V

ELECTION—
Of Co. Boards Pub. Inst.................... 15 32-34
For creating School Sub-District............ 16 37
Of Trustees of School Sub-Districts 16 37
ELECTORS—Of Sub-District. ....
Qualifications of.......................... 17 38
EXAMINATIONS FOR COUNTY CERTIFICATES—
Conducted by Co. Supt...................... 22 62
Applicants must file endorsement of good character...................................... 20 57
Applicants must pay a fee of $1.00.......... 20 51
Held semi-annually.......................... 22 60
Rules governing............................. 22 62
Method of procedure in...................... 23 63
Penalty for cheating in 22 62
Privilege of dissatisfied applicants........ 24 66
Papers to be preserved one year............. 24 66
Penalty for violating provisions of examination-laws.................................... 24 67
State Supt. may order special examinations .... 12 21 X
EXAMINATION FOR STATE CERTIFICATES—
Applicant must file endorsement and pay fee... 20 51
State Supt. to conduct...................... 12 21 X
EXAMINATION—
Fee.. 20 51
How applied................................ 24 65
EXAMINATION PAPERS—
Not to be signed........................... 23 63
Filed in Co. Supt's. office................ 24 66
Examinee may have published................ 24 66
EXAMINER—
Supt. may appoint assistant................ 22 63
EXAMINATION QUESTIONS—
Prepared by State Supt..................... 22 62
Sent under Seal, etc....................... 22 62
ESTIMATE, ITEMIZED—
See ITEMIZED ESTIMATE.

EXPENSES—Traveling of Board...............
   Must be itemized............................. 16 30
EXAMINATIONS—Public. of schools. ....
   When teacher must hold.................... 25 68   6

F.

FORFEITURES—
   Of school money............................ 26
   When county forfeits........................ 26 76
   When school forfeits........................ 26 77
   Disposition of forfeitures................... 26 76-77
FLORIDA NORMAL SCHOOL AND BUSINESS COLLEGE—
   Free tuition to pupil in each Senatorial Dist..... 29 93
   Beneficiaries, how appointed................. 29 93
FENSES—Around school ground..................
   Board to build and keep in repair. .... 13 28   V
FORMS—
   No. 1. Of commission of Co. Board of Pub. Inst. 49
   No. 2 Of appointment of members of Co. Board. 50
   No. 3. Of acceptance of appointment on Co. Bd. 50
   No. 4. Of removing member of Co. Board 51
   No. 5. Of recommending School Supervisor. ... 51
   No. 6. Of appointment of School Supervisor ... 52
   No. 7. Of acceptance of appointment of School Supervisor 52
   No. 8. Of endorsement of applicant for County examination 53
   No. 8. Of application for Ex. for State Certificate 53
   No. 10. Of recommendation for Life Certificates.. 54
   No. 11. Of application for Special Life Certificate 55
   No. 12. Of Teacher's Third Grade Certificate ... 55
   No. 13. Of Teacher's Second Grade Certificate.... 56
   No. 14. Of Teacher's First Grade Certificate 56
   No. 15. Of Teacher's State Certificate 57
   No. 16. Of Teacher's Life Certificate 58
   No. 17. Of Primary Life Certificate............. 59

FORMS—(Continued,)

    No. 18. Of suspension or revocation of certificate. 59
    No. 19. Of contract with teacher............ 60
    No. 20. Of decision of Board on charges against teacher............................ 61
    No. 21. Of notice of suspension of pupil........... 61
    No. 22. Of notice for called meeting of Board.... 62
    No. 23. Of Co. School Warrant................. 63
    No 24. Of notice to Comptroller............... 63
    No. 25. Of requisition on Comptroller......... 64
    No. 26. Of Bond of Trustees of Sub-District.... 64
    No. 27. Of contract for building a school-house.. 65
    No. 28. Of deed by husband and wife............ 66
    No. 29. Of itemized estimate.................. 68

FUNDS—State School........................
    See STATE SCHOOL FUND.

FUNDS—County School.........................
    See COUNTY SCHOOL FUND.

FURNITURE—
    Board to supply........................ 13 28 V
    Penalty for defacing................... 27 84

G.

GRADING—
    Committee............................. 23 64
    To be appointed by Co. Board.......... 15 30
    Duties and qualifications of.......... 23 64
    Time allowed, and conpensation for services.... 24 65
    Must return all papers to Co. Supt.......... 24 66
    Must conform to instructions sent out by State Supt......... 23 64

GRADATION SHEET—
    Grading committee make two copies........... 23 64

GROUNDS—
    Improvement and care of..................... 13 28 V
    Authority of teacher on.................... 25 68 IV

H.

HIGH SCHOOL—
    Boards to establish one in each county............ 14 28   V
    All qualified pupils of county may attend......... 46 17
HOLIDAYS... 26 74
    Legal holidays described, see note................ 26
    Attendance for, how recorded by teacher.......... 47 23
    Recommendations concerning observance of Christmas.. 45 13

I.

INSTITUTE FOR BLIND, DEAF AND DUMB....... 10
    Board of Managers of............................. 10 12
    Location... 10 13
    Beneficiaries and pay pupils..................... 10 14
    Application for, how made....................... 10 15
    County Commissioners to supply means of transportation to.................................... 10 16
    See also BOARD OF MANAGERS.
INSTITUTES—
    State Supt. shall provide for..................... 11 21   III
INSTITUTES, COUNTY -
    Examination fund may be used for................ 24 65
ITEMIZED ESTIMATE—
    For county school fund........................... 14 28   XIV
    For sub-district fund............................. 17 39
INTEREST ON COMMON SCHOOL FUND—
    See STATE SCHOOL FUND.
INCOMPETENCY—
    Cause for removal................................ 7 3   III

L.

LAW—
    Regulations of Co. Boards have effect of......... 43 2
LAWS—
    Session of 1893. See APPENDIX.
    Providing for uniform examinations.............. 31

LAWS—(Continued.)
 Providing for election of boards...... 35
 Providing for creation of sub-districts........... 37
 Ibid............................... 38
 Regulating school day, etc............... 40
 Concerning assessment and collection of revenue. 41
 Resolution proposing amendment to Constitution. 42
LANDS—
 See SCHOOL LANDS.
LECTURERS—
 Paid out of examination fund.......... 24 65
LOCATING SCHOOLS—
 Duty of board............................. 13 28 II
 Proviso concerning..... .... 14 28 VI
 Regulation concerning.......................... 46 16
LOST TIME—
 When may be made up 26 75
LIABILITY FOR LOSS—
 See OFFICERS.
LIFE CERTIFICATE—
 Statute concerning..... .... 21 56
 Valid anywhere in the State.................... 22 58
 Regulation concerning.......................... 48 30
 Form of..................... 58
LINE SCHOOLS—
 See ATTENDANCE.

M.

MONTH—
 See SCHOOL MONTH.
MONTHLY REPORT—
 See TEACHER.
MONEYS—
 Management and safe keeping of................. 8 8 I
 Apportioned by State Supt...................... 11 21 IV

MONEYS—(Continued.)

Discretionary powers of Supt. in	11	21	V
Of Sub-District, how applied	17	42	
Officers to give bond before receiving	18	42	

N.

NEGLECT OF DUTY—

Cause for removal	7	3	III

NORMAL SCHOOLS............................... 9

For whites	9	9
For negroes	10	11
Under control of State Board	9	1
Faculties, and how chosen	10	10

O.

OFFICERS—

Of Dept. Pub. Inst.	7	2	
Qualifications of	43	1	
Subject to regulations of department	7	3	I
Tenure of office, maximum	7	3	II
Subject to removal for cause	7	3	III
When required to give bond	8	6	II
When personally liable for loss	8	6	III
Must turn over effects	8	6	IV
General duties of	8	6	
Not to vote on fixing their own compensation	7	3	IV
Must use blanks prescribed	43	3	
Must not deal in text-books	28	87-88	

OUT BUILDINGS—

Board to provide	13	28	V

P.

PATRONS—

May recommend for Supervisor	47	26
Not authorized to employ or contract with teacher	44	8

PENALTIES—
  For cheating in examinations for Certificates. ... 22 62
  For violating examination laws 24 67
  For circulating obscene literature, etc........... 27 83
  For defacing school property.................... 27 84
  For insulting teacher in presence of pupils...... 27 85
  For injuring school property........... ....,28 85
  For school officers dealing in text-books, etc..... 28 87–88
  For disturbing school 28 89
PUNISHMENT—
  Must not be unnecessarily severe .... 25 68   IV
  Teacher may inflict corporal punishment 47 28
PUPILS—
  Duties of teacher toward.......... .... 24 68 I-IV
  May be suspended......... .... 25 68   V
  Must attend their own district school.... ...... 46 17
  Non-resident may be charged tuition 45 15
  From adjoining counties 26 78
PRIMARY LIFE CERTIFICATE—
  Provisions concerning....................,...... 22 56
  Good anywhere in the State 22 58
  Application for, how made..... .... 48 31
  Form of application 54
  Form of certificate........................... 59

Q.

QUALIFICATIONS—
  Of school officers. See OFFICERS.
  Of teachers. See TEACHERS.
QUORUM—
  What shall constitute.......................... 7 5
QUESTIONS FOR EXAMINATION—
  See EXAMINATION QUESTIONS.

R.

RECEIPTS—
To be taken by retiring officer .... 8　6　IV

REMOVAL OF SUBORDINATE OFFICERS—
State Board has the power of .... 9　8　IV
Cause for .... 7　3　II

RENT—
County Board may rent for school use .... 13　28　V

RECORDS AND ACCOUNTS—
County Boards must keep .... 14　28　IX
County Supt. must keep .... 18　44　II

REGISTERS, TEACHERS'—
Teachers must use prescribed register .... 43　3
Register must be kept in accordance with directions .... 44　6
Teacher must procure before beginning school ... 47　27
To be delivered to Supervisor at close of school ... 25　68　VII

REGULATIONS—
County boards should adopt and print .... 45　12
Have force of law .... 43　2

REGULATIONS OF DEPARTMENT OF PUBLIC INSTRUCTION 43–48
Duties of officers concerning .... 7　3　I
Concerning eligibility to office .... 43　1
Concerning regulations of Co. Boards .... 43　2
Concerning use of prescribed blanks .... 43　3
Concerning Co. Boards of Pub. Inst .... 44　4-17
Concerning Co. Supt. Pub. Inst .... 46　18-23
Concerning supervisors .... 37　24-26
Concerning teachers .... 47　27-28
Concerning teachers' certificates .... 48　29-32

REPORTS—
Seminary visitors to make .... 28　91
State Supt. to make .... 12　21　XII
Co. Boards to make .... 14　28　IX
Trustees sub-district to make .... 17　40

INDEX. 83

REPORTS—(Continued.)
Co. Supt. to make....... 46 19
To State Dept., term embraced in .. 25 70
Teacher's, how made. 47 27

S.

SCHOOLS, FREE PUBLIC—
To be established and maintained............ 7 1
Under general management of State Supt........ 11 20
Under special management of County Board.... 47 25
Minimum annual term..... 13 28 II
Sha'l be located by County Board.......... 13 28 II
Duty of County Board to Grade............. 14 28 X
Time of opening schools fixed by Co. Board........ 25 71
When schools for any year may begin.......... 25 72
When schools for any year must close..... 25 71
Penalty for disturbing 28 89

SCHOOL AGE—
Defined......... 7 1

SCHOOL BOARD DISTRICTS—
Provisions concerning .. 15 32

SCHOOL DAY—
Defined within limits.......... 25 73 I
Fixed by County Boards... 15 31
Number in school months........ 25 73 II

SCHOOL DISTRICT—
See DISTRICT, PERMANENT.

SCHOOL EXAMINATION, PUBLIC—
Teacher must hold at close of term.... 25 63 VI

SCHOOL-HOUSE—
Warmed and kept in order by........ 13 28 V
Penalty for defacing.... 27 84

SCHOOL LANDS—
Control and management of........ 3 3 I

SCHOOL LAW—
Printing and distribution of.... 11 21 I

SCHOOL LEVY—
   For County............................ 15 28 XIV
   For Sub-district........................ 17 39
SCHOOL MONTH—
   Defined................................ 25 73 II
   Teacher's report for must contain 20 days....... 47 23
SCHOOL PROPERTY—
   Title vested in whom.................... 13 24
SCHOOL SITE—
   Co. Board to select, requirements, etc......... 13 28 IV
   Board may contract with members for.......... 15 29
SCHOOL SUB-DISTRICT—
   See SUB-DISTRICT.
SCHOOL SUPERVISORS—
   See SUPERVISORS.
SCHOOL YEAR—
   Defined................................ 25 70
   May contain two terms.................... 25 73 IV
SEAL—
   State Supt. to have...................... 12 21 VIII
SEMINARIES—
   Visitors to report to State Supt............. 28 91
   State Supt. to visit and report.............. 12 21 XII
   Beneficiaries of......................... 28 90
STATE BOARD OF EDUCATION—
   Personnel and powers of.................. 8 9
   Have charge of school lands............... 8 8 I
   Management of State School Fund........... 9 8 II
   May entertain appeals................... 9 8 III
   May remove subordinate officers............ 9 8 IV
   To foster higher education................ 9 8 V
   To co-operate with State Supt............. 9 8 VI
   Shall invest School Fund................. 9 8 VII
   Fill vacancies on School Board............. 9 8 VIII
   Have charge of Normal Schools............ 9 9
   Are Bord of Managers of Inst. for Blind and Deaf. 10 12
   State Supt. Secretary of.................. 8 7

STATE CERTIFICATE—

How and by whom issued.................... 12	21	X
Provisions concerning..................... 21	55	
Valid any when in State.................... 22	58	
Regulations concerning endorsement.......... 48	29	
Form of application for examination for...... 53		
Form of Certificate......................... 57		

STATE SUPERINTENDENT OF PUBLIC INSTRUCTION—

Is Secretary of State Board of Education...... 8	7	
Has general oversight of schools............. 11	20	
Special duties............................... 11	21	
To prepare and distribute necessary forms, blanks, etc............................... 11	21	I
To call conventions of school officers......... 11	21	II
To hold teacher's institutes................. 11	21	III
To apportion School Fund................... 11	21	IV-V
To entertain and decide or refer appeals...... 11	21	VI
To prescribe rules and regulations for Dept. of Education.................................. 12	21	VII
To have a seal of office..................... 12	21	VIII
Residence and office of..................... 12	21	IX
To prepare questions for examinations......... 12	21	X
To conduct examinations for State certificates... 12	21	X
To grant life and special life certificates...... 12	21	X
To nominate to fill vacancies on School Boards.. 12	21	XI
To visit seminaries and report................ 12	21	XII

SUB-DISTRICTS—

General regulations for creating............... 16	37	
How abolished............................... 18	43	
May own school property..................... 13	28	I
See also TRUSTEES.		

SUPERVISORS OF SCHOOLS—   9   46-47

Appointed by Co. Board..................... 13	28	III
To have oversight of schools................. 19	46	I
To report monthly........................... 20	46	II
To have charge of buildings, repairs, etc....... 20	46	III
To co-operate with teacher................... 20	46	IV

SUPERVISORS OF SCHOOLS—(Continued.)

To take census	20	47
Office one of oversight, not control	47	25
May recommend teachers	44	8
Under direction of Co. Board	47	24
Form of recommendation for	51	
Form of appointment of	52	
Form of acceptance of appointment	52	
Regulations concerning	47	24-26

T.

TAX, COUNTY SCHOOL—

Estimated by Co. Board	14	28	XIV
Levied by County Commissioners	15	28	XIV
Not to exceed 5 mills	15	28	XIV

TAX, SUB-DISTRICT—

Regulations concerning	17	39

TEACHER—

Duties of	24	68 I-VIII
Whom the board may employ as	44	7
Exempt from military and jury duty	25	69
When not entitled to compensation	44	7
Duties concerning Arbor Day	45	14
Regulations concerning	47	27-28
Penalty for insulting	27	85
Not to deal in school books	28	87
Penalty for	28	88

TREASURER OF CO. BOARD 13 57

Duties of	26	79
All county school moneys go to	27	81

TRUSTEES OF AG. COLLEGE—

Make annual report to State Supt.	30	96

TRUSTEES OF SUB-DISTRICTS—

Election of	17	37
General duties of	17	39
Special duties of	17	40

TRUSTEES OF SUB-DISTRICTS—*(Continued.)*
   Powers of 17 41-42
   Must give bond 18 42
   Form of bond of 64
TEXT BOOKS—
   School officers may not deal in 28 87
   Penalty for violation of above 28 88

V.

VISITORS—
   See SEMINARIES.
VACANCIES—
   How filled on School Boards .... 9 8 VIII
   In schools, Co. Supt. may fill 47 22
VOTERS—
   See ELECTORS.

W.

WARRANTS—County schools ....
   Form of 23

Y.

YEAR—
   See SCHOOL YEAR.

www.ingramcontent.com/pod-product-compliance
Lightning Source LLC
Chambersburg PA
CBHW020308090426
42735CB00009B/1264